VIRGINIA MILITIA COMMANDERS at YORKTOWN

VIRGINIA MILITIA COMMANDERS *at* YORKTOWN

SEAN M. HEUVEL

THE History PRESS

Published by The History Press
An imprint of Arcadia Publishing
Charleston, SC
www.historypress.com

Copyright © 2025 by Sean M. Heuvel
All rights reserved

Front cover: A depiction by Keith Rocco of the ceremonial surrender of Cornwallis's Army on October 19, 1781, following the Siege of Yorktown. *Colonial National Historical Park.*

First published 2025

Manufactured in the United States

ISBN 9781467159715

Library of Congress Control Number: 2025941127

Notice: The information in this book is true and complete to the best of our knowledge. It is offered without guarantee on the part of the author or The History Press. The author and The History Press disclaim all liability in connection with the use of this book.

All rights reserved. No part of this book may be reproduced or transmitted in any form whatsoever without prior written permission from the publisher except in the case of brief quotations embodied in critical articles and reviews.

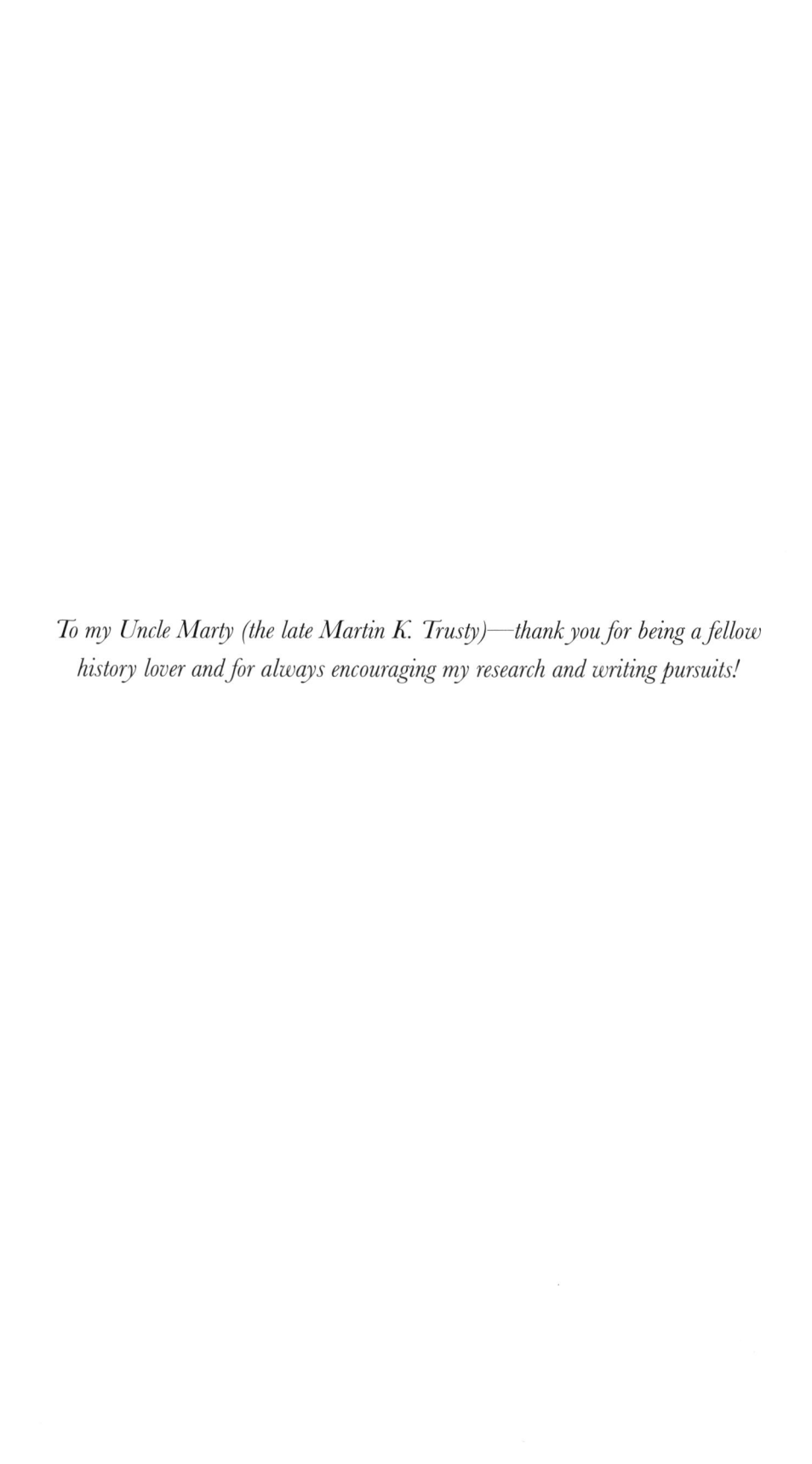

To my Uncle Marty (the late Martin K. Trusty)—thank you for being a fellow history lover and for always encouraging my research and writing pursuits!

Contents

Acknowledgements 9
Preface 11
Introduction 17

1. Lieutenant Colonel James Baytop 27
2. Colonel Lewis Burwell 30
3. Colonel Charles Dabney 32
4. Lieutenant Colonel William Darke 37
5. Colonel Elias Edmonds Jr. 43
6. Lieutenant Colonel William Fontaine 45
7. Colonel William Griffin 49
8. Colonel James Innes 51
9. Brigadier General Robert Lawson 55
10. Colonel William Lewis 60
11. Colonel Reuben Lindsay 63
12. Colonel Sampson Mathews 65
13. Lieutenant Colonel Thomas Mathews 70
14. Lieutenant Colonel John Francis Mercer 73
15. Colonel Thomas Meriwether 77

Contents

16. Brigadier General Thomas Nelson Jr. 79
17. Colonel William Nelson 85
18. Colonel John Page 87
19. Colonel Sir John Peyton 91
20. Colonel Beverley Randolph 93
21. Colonel Holt Richeson 95
22. Lieutenant Colonel Henry Skipwith 98
23. Brigadier General Edward Stevens 101
24. Lieutenant Colonel St. George Tucker 107
25. Colonel Samuel Vance 113
26. Lieutenant Colonel John Webb 115
27. Brigadier General George Weedon 118
28. Lieutenant Colonel George West 127

Appendix A. Chronology of the Siege of Yorktown 129
Appendix B. Partial List of Virginia Militia Units Present
    at the Siege of Yorktown 131
Appendix C. Virginia Militia Casualties at the
    Siege of Yorktown 135
Appendix D. Virginia Militia Commanders at the
    Siege of Yorktown 137
Appendix E. Virginia Militia Commanders at the
    Siege of Yorktown Who Are Eligible for Representation
    in the Society of the Cincinnati (Based Upon Prior
    Continental Army Service) 139
Bibliography 141
Index 155
About the Author 160

Acknowledgements

I am indebted to a number of people and organizations for their help in creating this book, particularly as the subject matter has not been examined extensively within the realm of existing Revolutionary War historiography. First and foremost, the members of the Williamsburg (Virginia) Chapter of the Sons of the American Revolution—particularly John Lynch and Gary Dunaway—were enthusiastic supporters who contributed vital research assistance in the project's early stages. The staff of the American Revolution Institute of the Society of the Cincinnati provided vital encouragement and support as well. I am also indebted to the Colonial Williamsburg Foundation's John D. Rockefeller Jr. Library for its rich collection of books and other materials that were critical to this book's development. The Jamestown-Yorktown Foundation, the Virginia Museum of History & Culture, George Washington's Mount Vernon, Thomas Jefferson's Monticello and the National Park Service were also highly useful organizational resources. Further, Biddie Shelor of the King and Queen County Historical Society, Robert Kelly of the Gloucester County Museum of History, Rick Armstrong of the Bath County Historical Society, Wayne Brooks of the Caroline County Historical Society and Suzanne Levy of the Fairfax County Historical Society all provided helpful guidance that informed my efforts to learn about officers who hailed from each of those areas. In a similar vein, Sue Kovach Shuman of the City of Fairfax Library provided additional vital research support, as did Bette Dillehay and Colanne Bunting with Mathews Memorial Library. Historian Michael Moore was also kind

Acknowledgements

enough to lend his expertise on the Siege of Yorktown, serving as a valued advisor for this project. Within the realm of illustrations, I am also grateful to Forrest Harris of Bicast Inc., who kindly provided permission to feature images in this book that are in his company's possession. Also, the digital collections of the National Portrait Gallery, the Library of Congress and the New York Public Library were invaluable sources for illustrations.

As with previous books I have had the privilege to write, the people of Christopher Newport University (CNU)—where I have had the good fortune to work for over twenty years—were indispensable in making this book a reality. For instance, Dr. Lynn Lambert and Dr. David Salomon encouraged me to continue in my writing, even after I returned to an administrative position at the university following many years of full-time faculty service. Meanwhile, Dr. Jonathan White served as a valued thought partner, helping me refine the book's purpose and scope. I also benefited from the holdings at CNU's Trible Library, where digital services librarian Johnnie Gray was most helpful in preparing images for use in this book. In addition, Kate Jenkins and Dr. John Rodrigue at The History Press were valued resources over the course of this project. Lastly, I am indebted to my family—particularly my wife, Katey; my son, S.J.; and my daughter, Emma, for their steadfast support of my research and writing endeavors. It truly takes a village to create a work such as this.

Preface

My journey to learn more about the Virginia militia commanders who served during the Siege of Yorktown began several years ago. While undertaking some genealogical research, I discovered a pair of relatives from the Shenandoah Valley who served together at Yorktown as militia privates. My excitement abounded as I tried to imagine them operating in and around the siege lines during those fateful days in October 1781. As a military historian, I then grew interested in learning more about their company and regiment and how they fit into the broader Allied order of battle. Moreover, I was eager to learn about their commanding officers in an effort to get a more complete picture of their service. To my chagrin, I quickly discovered that information pertaining to Virginia militia forces at Yorktown was limited, to say the least. While in comparison, extensive information was available about the French and Continental Army units who served there, details about the militia were scarce. This was shocking and disappointing to me, as the Virginia militia constituted about 40 percent of the total Allied force at Yorktown. Nevertheless, it was also understandable, as detailed militia records were not always maintained during the frenzy of the siege, with militia units constantly coming and going. Moreover, some of the records that did exist were lost during the Civil War, as many local courthouses and government buildings were destroyed in the fighting. Ultimately, it dawned on me that there was a real void in existing Revolutionary War scholarship on this topic, and I wanted to do what I could to help fill it.

The Dawn of Peace on the morning of the surrender at Yorktown. *Library of Congress.*

As a lifelong student of leadership, my thoughts continued to turn to the individuals who commanded these militia units. Who were they? An examination of published sources revealed only the names of the commander in chief of Virginia forces, Brigadier General Thomas Nelson Jr. (who was also Virginia's governor), and his three brigade commanders: Brigadier General Robert Lawson, Brigadier General Edward Stevens and Brigadier General George Weedon. However, hardly any information was available about the regimental commanders and other senior officers who helped compose this force. It then occurred to me that this was how I could help fill in some of the aforementioned information gap: by telling the stories of these leaders. To be sure, the stories of *all* the patriot militiamen who served at Yorktown are important. However, given the scope of existing information, I decided to focus on the senior commanders, as I believed more details about them would be readily available.

But how could I track down the identities of these "missing" militia officers? The answer resided in a veritable primary source treasure trove that is available to Revolutionary War historians: postwar pension application records. I began searching, poring through the digitized pension records made available by the Southern Campaigns Revolutionary War Pension

Statements & Rosters database. By performing different combinations of keyword searches, I looked for patterns where multiple veterans identified the same senior officers as being present at the siege. To my frustration, there were sometimes instances where only a single source claimed that a particular officer was present in or around Yorktown. If I could not corroborate such claims with additional primary sources, I opted not to include those officers in this book. Instead, I included only senior officers—primarily lieutenant colonels, colonels and brigadier generals—who were identified as being present at the siege by multiple veterans, as reported in their postwar pension applications. For the purposes of this work, I also focused on the senior commanders who were there during the actual siege, which dated from September 28 to October 19, 1781. While many militia commanders came and went in the weeks leading up to that fateful event, I wanted to emphasize the leaders who were physically present within those specific dates.

What emerged from this research was a list of nearly thirty militia commanders who have mostly been lost to history. While some names are certainly recognizable to Revolutionary War historians and enthusiasts, most of them are little known to modern readers. As I studied their lives and wartime service, interesting patterns began to emerge that offered deeper insights into their Revolutionary War contributions. For instance, several of the officers had served on the Continental Line during the war's earlier stages, thereby seeing action in some of the conflict's most legendary battles. For a variety of reasons, they had decided to leave the Continental Army but still had a desire to serve, albeit closer to home, that usually manifested itself in their appointment as militia officers. Meanwhile, other militia commanders at Yorktown were civic leaders who became officers because of their standing in the community. These individuals were typically county lieutenants or legislators who rallied with their fellow residents to defend Virginia from pending British attack. Moreover, many of these leaders contributed personal funds to help equip their units for service—often to the detriment of their own financial well-being. Thus, these militia commanders were all ardent patriots fighting for freedom from the British—which is interesting to consider as the vast majority were also slaveowners. This represents a fundamental conundrum that certainly merits further discussion, analysis and reflection. At the time, these patriots fought for liberty as they conceptualized it, and even if unwittingly, they planted a seed by their actions that would help advance that cause of freedom in later generations. Following the war, some of these officers returned to private life at home, like Cincinnatus,

Preface

A fanciful depiction of Lord Cornwallis surrendering his sword to General Washington. *New York Public Library.*

while others pursued long and varied public service careers. Several of the officers became members of Congress, governors or event close confidants of U.S. presidents. Thus, while many of these militia commanders long ago faded from public memory, they all made substantial contributions to the war effort as well as to the new republic and should be acknowledged for their efforts. *Virginia Militia Commanders at Yorktown* is therefore an attempt to shine a light on this distinguished group of leaders.

Ultimately, this book is not intended to be an all-encompassing list of every senior Virginia militia officer who served at the Siege of Yorktown. The fog of time and the limitations of existing information make achieving that goal difficult. Instead, it profiles a critical mass of these officers and endeavors to provide an opening salvo for what will hopefully be continued research on the topic. Undoubtedly, more exciting discoveries about this group will be made as additional information is discovered. As much as we know about the American Revolution, topics such as this remind us that there is always more to learn. And only through diligent research and focus can we continue to expand the frontier of knowledge in this area. Rededicating ourselves to this work will also enable us to get a more comprehensive picture of the Revolutionary War and its impact on all Americans. Let us continue this journey toward a more perfect union that these patriot forebears began for us along the siege lines at Yorktown.

Sean M. Heuvel, PhD
Williamsburg, Virginia

Introduction

The Siege of Yorktown represents one of the most iconic and important chapters in American history. Those fateful weeks in the fall of 1781 culminated in a crucial turning point in the American Revolution, forever changing the course of the war. The siege has also long been commemorated in the annals of American history, through scores of paintings, books and celebratory events. However, for as much as we know about this pivotal moment in the American story, there are still critical gaps in our collective knowledge. For instance, the contributions of Virginia militia forces to the siege are comparatively little known, even as we continue to advance into the twenty-first century. Although these men and the officers who led them constituted approximately 40 percent of the total Allied force, their stories have, in most cases, been lost to time. As discussed in the preface, *Virginia Militia Commanders at Yorktown* profiles many of the senior officers who commanded Virginia militia forces during the Siege of Yorktown. This topic is an important one, for it tells the story of the leaders who helped forge not just the Commonwealth but also the nation as a whole. Specifically, this book profiles nearly thirty such officers, who hailed from all corners of Virginia as well as parts of modern-day West Virginia. They came from a variety of backgrounds, ranging from planters to educators to lawyers to tavernkeepers. By the time they arrived at Yorktown, some were experienced battlefield commanders, while others were new to the military service arena. And following the war, some returned to private life, while others pursued long and distinguished careers in the field of public service. They all lived lives of consequence and merit further study.

Introduction

However, before embarking on the journey to learn more about their lives and times, it is important to take a step back in order to provide some context, as important questions need to be addressed. In particular, what was the role of the Virginia militia during the Yorktown Campaign? How was it organized, and what did it do to assist in the war effort? Moreover, who composed this force that ultimately found itself stationed near the siege lines at Yorktown? The study of the Virginia militia is significant, for by this time it constituted the only Virginia-based force operating in the Commonwealth. According to historian J.T. McAllister, who published one of the first major studies on this topic in 1913, the role of the Virginia militia during the American Revolution evolved over the course of the war. During the conflict's earlier stages, Virginia was able to raise and equip a number of Continental Line regiments, as it had not yet been attacked or occupied to any great extent by the enemy. That left militia forces with the sole tasks of guarding the frontier and defending the coasts. However, following the disastrous American defeats at the Siege of Charleston and the Battle of the Waxhaws, the Virginia Continental Line had largely ceased to exist. It was therefore up to the militia, a smattering of state troops and whatever Continental forces could be brought in from the outside to defend Virginia from increasing British aggression. Thus, while the Virginia militia are often overlooked in Revolutionary War scholarship, they played a vital role during these later stages of the war.

Historian William W. Reynolds did some of the seminal research on this topic that helps address the aforementioned questions. He published his findings in the aptly titled article "The Virginia Militia at the Siege of Yorktown," which appeared in the summer 2015 issue of *Military Collector & Historian*. It is a seminal work for any serious student of the subject. According to Reynolds, sixty of Virginia's seventy-five counties supplied militia forces that would ultimately be stationed in either Yorktown or Gloucester. The largest numbers came from the Shenandoah Valley, central Virginia, southside Virginia and northern Virginia, as the far western counties were too far away to contribute and the eastern counties were effectively blocked by advancing British forces. Over 70 percent of these men were drafted, and their ages ranged from around fifteen to over fifty-one. Furthermore, Reynolds explained that with the exception of the youngest militiamen, a majority took to the field with some degree of prior military service. Nearly 10 percent had even served for a time on the Continental Line and seen action in the war's northern campaigns. Many of these militiamen had seen action in the recent Battle of Guilford Courthouse, which was fought

INTRODUCTION

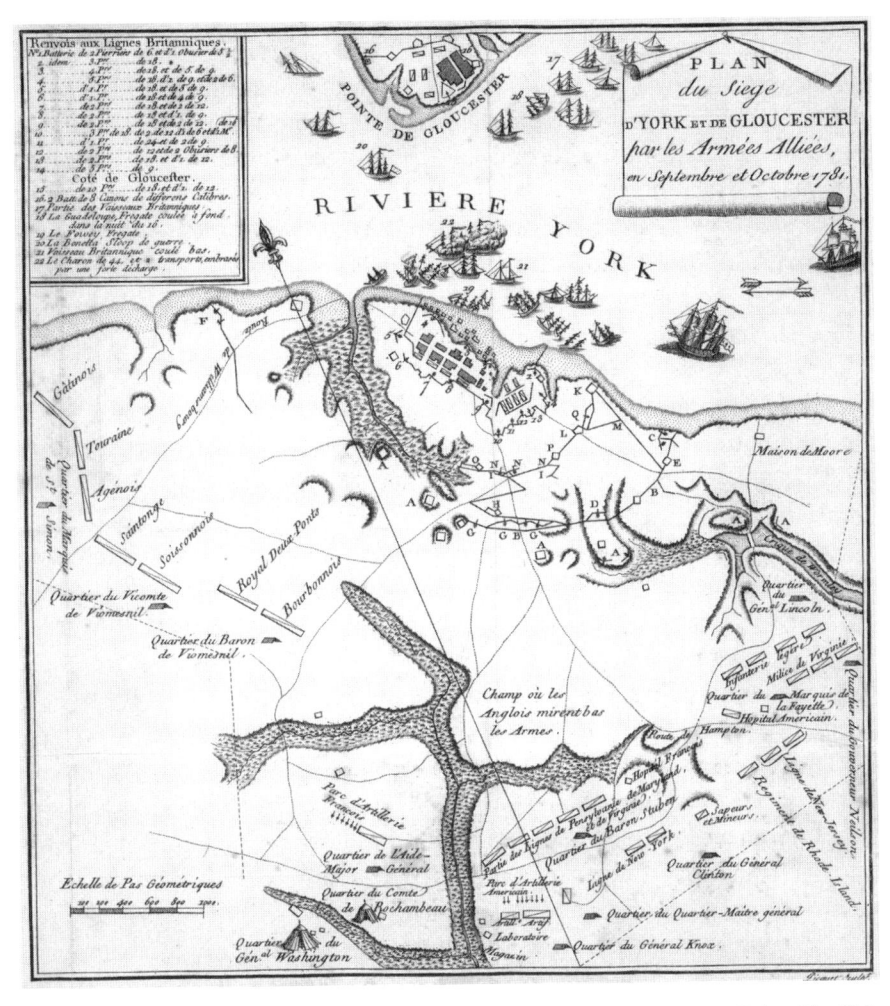

A French period map displaying the siege plan for Yorktown and Gloucester Point. *New York Public Library.*

on March 15, 1781. As the British threat in Virginia grew, calls for militia went out in July 1781, and forces trickled in over the next few weeks. Owing to the urgency of the situation, an additional call went out in late August, generating even more turnout. According to Reynolds, by September 26, 1781, nearly 3,800 militiamen had reached the Allied Army, and more were en route. Two days later, these forces began the twelve-mile march from Williamsburg to Yorktown; Colonel William Lewis and his Campbell County militiamen helped compose the army's advance elements. Once all the militia forces reached Yorktown with the rest of the army, they then went

Introduction

to work organizing camps, performing reconnaissance and skirmishing with the British. Reynolds noted that the Virginia militia encamped with the rest of the American Army on the right side of the Allied position. Specifically, they were located on the second line behind the Continental Army near Wormley Creek.

Estimates of the number of militiamen who were present during the Siege of Yorktown vary widely. For instance, in *The Guns of Independence: The Siege of Yorktown, 1781*, author Jerome Greene lists the total Virginia militia strength as 5,535 men (including 1,500 in Brigadier General George Weedon's brigade, 1,600 in Brigadier General Edward Stevens's brigade and 1,640 in Brigadier General Robert Lawson's brigade). Reynolds placed the total number of militiamen at approximately 4,000. Meanwhile, other historians, including Henry P. Johnston in his work *The Yorktown Campaign and the Surrender of Cornwallis* and Brendan Morrissey in *Yorktown 1781: The World Turned Upside Down*, have estimated the total number of militia to be closer to 3,000 (1,500 in Brigadier General George Weedon's brigade and a further 750 each in Brigadier General Edward Stevens's and Brigadier General Robert Lawson's brigades). Nell Moore Lee also lists those numbers in her biography of Brigadier General Thomas Nelson, *Patriot Above Profit*. Furthermore, this number is corroborated by Lieutenant Colonel St. George Tucker, who noted in his wartime journal that around September 27, there were about 3,000 militia in the field. The discrepancy in information about troop numbers is problematic yet understandable, considering there was a lot of coming and going of units during that time. Furthermore, while Continental and French Army officials kept meticulous records for their forces, recordkeeping among militia forces was nowhere near as thorough. For the purposes of this book, the estimated numbers listed by Johnston, Lee and Morrissey are utilized.

The militia forces at Yorktown played somewhat different roles than their counterparts in Gloucester. In the days leading up to the siege, Colonel Tucker noted that many militiamen were tasked with guarding roads and passes in the area between Williamsburg and Yorktown. However, as the siege commenced, a primary task for Yorktown-based militia was the construction of earthworks and redoubts, developed in conjunction with French and Continental forces. Between late September and early October, militiamen assisted in everything from cutting down trees to digging trenches. According to Colonel Tucker, General Lawson's entire brigade and much of General Stevens's brigade assisted in this effort. Such work was frequently done under British fire, and small numbers of militiamen were

Introduction

either wounded or killed in the process. According to Reynolds, following Allied assaults on British lines, militia forces also formed fatigue parties to rework captured redoubts and develop communication lines. Reynolds also noted that this is where some militia veterans likely came up with postwar tales of having "stormed" Redoubts 9 and 10 alongside the French and Continental forces. Along with digging trenches and building fortifications, Virginia militia played an invaluable role supporting the American artillery. According to Reynolds's research, in late September, a detachment of 250 militiamen was sent to Trebell's Landing, about six miles west of Yorktown, to assist in the offloading of artillery and ammunition from ships docked along the James River. Owing to manpower limitations in the Continental artillery, then Brigadier General Henry Knox also requested militia support in operating the vast array of siege cannon. Consequently, Brigadier General Thomas Nelson detached approximately 160 militiamen to help with such tasks as constructing batteries, transporting ammunition and cleaning the cannons. These militiamen were therefore a key force multiplier for General Knox and his artillerists. Meanwhile, militiamen in Gloucester tended to be more mobile and, in the case of Lieutenant Colonel John Francis Mercer and his grenadier militia, actually saw action against the British at the Battle of the Hook.

Continental artillery in position along the siege lines at Yorktown. *Bicast Inc., Walter Miller.*

A depiction of the British surrender at Yorktown on October 19, 1781. *Library of Congress.*

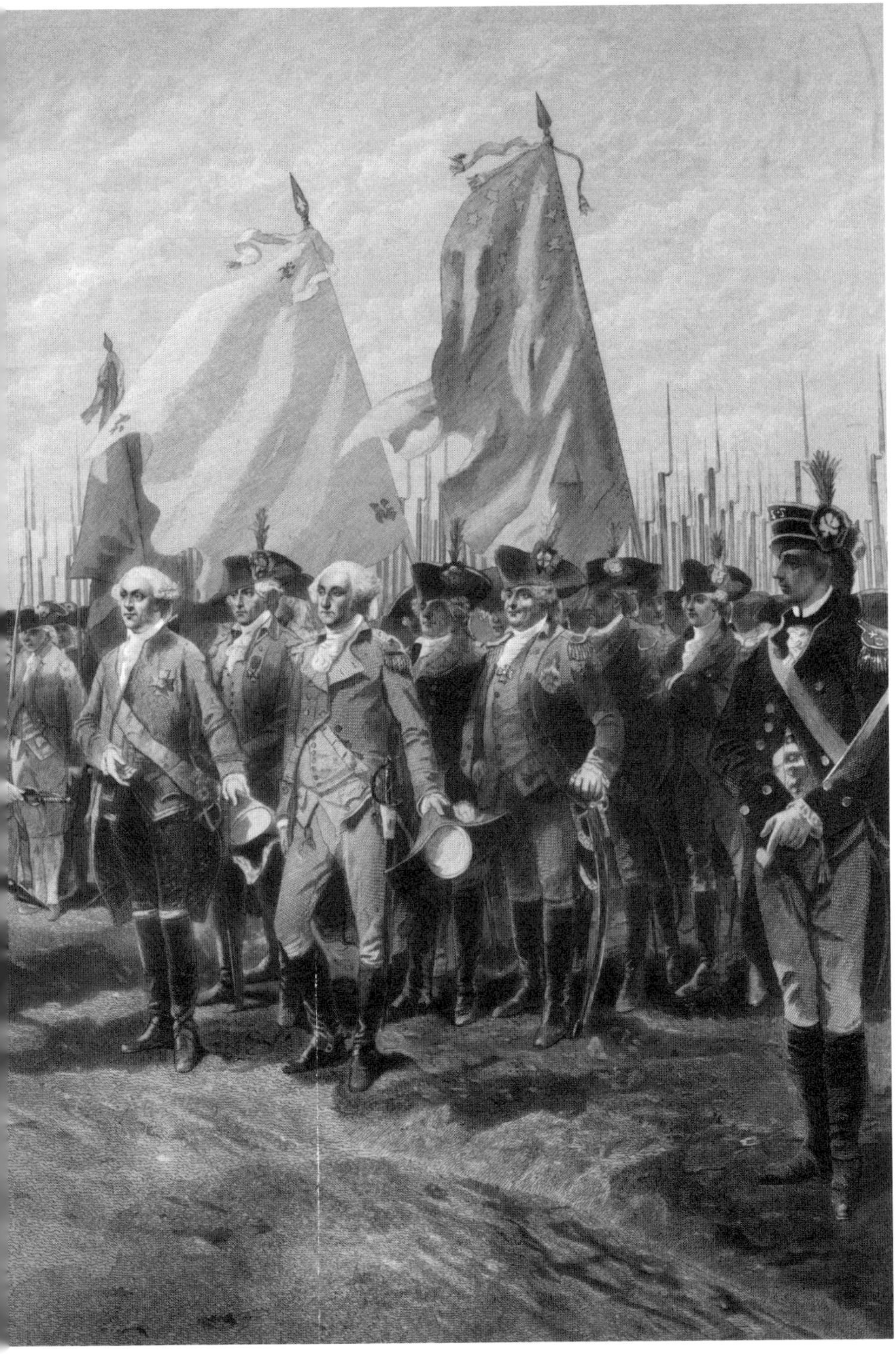

Introduction

According to Reynolds, militia forces were used for a variety of additional tasks during the Siege of Yorktown. Foremost among them were the dual responsibilities of scouting and sharpshooting. Prior to and during the siege, parties of militia were placed in key positions around Yorktown to monitor British movements. Similarly, militiamen played an important role in reconnoitering the British positions at Gloucester Point. As many of these backwoods militiamen were excellent marksmen, their services were also utilized to harass British troops along the siege lines. Owing to the logistical challenges of supporting an Allied army that numbered in the thousands, militia forces were also active in quartermaster and medical support roles. Several militiamen, experienced as teamsters, drove supply wagons that went on to support the Allied troops. They also transported the wounded to local field hospitals and even helped provide care for the patients. In one or two isolated cases, qualified militiamen were even mobilized to serve as surgeons.

Following the British surrender, Virginia militia forces participated in the ceremonies on October 19. In Yorktown, the tattered militiamen were positioned to the rear of the Continental forces, both formations striking a marked contrast to the smartly uniformed French troops. A short time later, militia forces commanded by Colonel Mercer assisted the French in the British surrender ceremony at Gloucester Point. With victory now complete, many of the militiamen were discharged and sent home. However, following a few days of well-deserved rest, 1,900 militia commanded by Brigadier General Robert Lawson were assigned the task of escorting approximately 7,500 British Army prisoners to internment camps. General Washington desired to get the prisoners moved inland as quickly as possible in order to avoid a possible British rescue from the coast. Departing Yorktown on October 21, the large formation traveled north to camps in Winchester, Virginia, and Frederick, Maryland, where the prisoners were deposited in early November. The escorting militia forces were subsequently able to transfer the prisoners over to militia based in those areas at that time. These militiamen were then able to return to their homes and conclude their part in one of the war's most defining chapters. In later years, many of them would apply for pensions as elderly men, prompting them to tell their stories one last time to the best of their abilities. While the fog of time and advanced age sometimes led to digressions from reality, these recollections became critical tools in helping preserve the stories of these individuals and their collective contributions to the war effort.

Overall, the Virginia militia played a vital and multifaceted role in the Allied victory at Yorktown, and the stories of the thousands of individuals

Introduction

who composed this force deserve to be commemorated and remembered. Returning to the central premise of this book, a small step toward that larger goal is to explore the lives and service of the senior officers who helped lead them. While a few of these officers are well known to Revolutionary War historians and even, in some cases, to the public at large, many others have largely disappeared from our collective memory. What follows is a series of biographical sketches intended to help bring these militia officers back into focus. They are followed by appendices that provide further context about these individuals as well as the role played by Virginia militia at Yorktown in general. This information will, hopefully, serve as a catalyst for additional research that will provide even more insights as we seek to learn more about this important component of our Revolutionary generation.

Chapter 1

LIEUTENANT COLONEL JAMES BAYTOP
(1754–1822)

James Baytop was born in 1754 to a family that had long been situated in Gloucester County. The Baytops immigrated to America from Kent, England, in the mid-seventeenth century and thereafter resided at their family estate in Gloucester, known as Springfield. Baytop's father, also named James, served as the tobacco inspector for Gloucester County prior to his passing in 1766. He was later succeeded in that role by another son. The younger James Baytop went on to establish his residence at Barren Point along the York River and would marry three times over the course of his lifetime, having a total of five children.

Baytop rallied to the patriot cause at the outset of the American Revolution and was appointed a first lieutenant in the Seventh Virginia Regiment on March 7, 1776. In that capacity, he likely saw action at the Battles of Brandywine and Germantown. Following a promotion to captain on December 11, 1777, Baytop transferred to the Fifth Virginia Regiment on September 14, 1778, before tendering his resignation from the Continental Army on May 12, 1779. However, like other former Continental Line officers, he found ways to continue his service to the revolutionary cause. On February 1, 1781, Colonel John Page recommended to Governor Thomas Jefferson that Baytop receive a commission as a lieutenant colonel in the Gloucester County militia, which took effect shortly thereafter. During the Siege of Yorktown, Baytop went on to serve as second in command of Page's Gloucester County militia regiment, which was part of Brigadier General George Weedon's brigade. Baytop and his troops spent much of that time

A Society of the Cincinnati diploma similar to the one that would have been issued to Lieutenant Colonel James Baytop. *New York Public Library.*

shadowing British forces, encamping temporarily at such places as Ware Church and Gloucester Courthouse. While they remained ready for a major British attack, the surrender at Yorktown brought an end to any threat of such an incursion.

Following the war, Baytop returned to Barren Point and continued his career in public service. In the 1790s, he served in the Virginia House of Delegates and was also part of a committee to help settle the accounts of the Gloucester County sheriff, Colonel Sir John Peyton. By that time, his Barren Point estate was assessed at over one thousand acres. On June 9, 1792, Baytop petitioned for increased arms for Gloucester and Mathews County, as he feared a possible slave revolt similar to one that had taken place on the Eastern Shore. In 1796, he also became an original member of the Society of the Cincinnati. Baytop briefly resumed his military career in 1799 by gaining appointment as a major in the Seventh Virginia Infantry. However, he was honorably discharged in June the following year. Around 1806, Baytop moved to Elizabeth City County (modern-day Hampton), where he built a house on a farm called Goodwood. Financial problems may have facilitated this move from Gloucester. Baytop's final foray into public service occurred when he was appointed a county justice in 1816.

In 1818, he continued to be in reduced financial circumstances, owning only a small plot with twenty-seven acres of uncultivated land along with a small property in King and Queen County. Mounting debts prompted him to apply for a pension in April that year. Friends and allies claimed that the debts did not stem from want of exertion but rather from the necessity of having to support a large family. Baytop's request for a pension was later approved, and he was granted twenty dollars per month for two years of service as a captain on the Virginia Continental Line. Baytop passed away in 1822, and his place of burial is unknown. His great-grandnephew was Confederate Brigadier General William Booth Taliaferro.

Chapter 2

COLONEL LEWIS BURWELL

(1745-1800)

Lewis Burwell was born on September 26, 1745, in Williamsburg, Virginia. A son of Armistead and Christian (Blair) Burwell, he descended from the prominent Burwell family that had long been situated in the Williamsburg and James City County areas. His grandfather Colonel Lewis Burwell III established the 1,400-acre Kingsmill Plantation in the mid-1730s, which went on to become one of the grandest of the James River plantations. In the 1750s, another Burwell relative built nearby Carter's Grove, which was considered one of the most beautiful homes in America. Burwell spent his refined youth in the Williamsburg area, where he obtained a classical education and interacted with such notables as Thomas Jefferson, Patrick Henry and George Washington. In 1768, he married Anne Spotswood, a scion of another prominent Tidewater family and a granddaughter of Virginia Governor Alexander Spotswood. A short time later, they moved to what was then a frontier area of Mecklenburg County and established their own plantation, called Stoneland, where they proceeded to raise twelve children. In this new home, they re-created the opulent lifestyle to which they had grown accustomed in Williamsburg. Over the next three decades, Burwell would acquire over 9,000 acres in Mecklenburg, Lunenburg and Franklin Counties, becoming a major political and military leader in the area.

At the dawn of the American Revolution, Burwell was serving as the chief military officer in Mecklenburg County, and therefore, he engaged

President William Henry Harrison (*shown here*) was a cousin of Colonel Lewis Burwell's second wife, Elizabeth Harrison Burwell. *Library of Congress.*

in militia service throughout the conflict, commanding forces from Mecklenburg as well as from Brunswick and Lunenburg Counties. As the war came to Virginia in early 1781, he mobilized militia forces in the area while warning Governor Thomas Jefferson of chronic weapons and ammunition shortages. A few months later, Burwell raised a regiment at his own expense, and under orders from Jefferson's successor, Governor Thomas Nelson, he and his men proceeded to march toward the developing Siege of Yorktown. They crossed the James River near Hog Island and passed through Williamsburg on the way to Yorktown. On reaching the area around September 30, 1781, he was immediately directed to Gloucester by Governor Nelson to reinforce Brigadier General George Weedon's brigade. Burwell's force therefore remained at Gloucester Point throughout the siege, helping counter the British forces who were fortified there. Following the war, Burwell went on to serve in the Virginia General Assembly for fourteen years. He was also an original member of the Society of the Cincinnati. After his first wife's death, he married Elizabeth Harrison, who was a cousin of future President William Henry Harrison. Burwell and his second wife went on to raise another four children at Stoneland, which by then was the largest home in southside Virginia. He passed away at Stoneland on July 1, 1800, at the age of fifty-four, leaving behind a large family that continued to serve in prominent civic and military roles within the region. U.S. Marine Corps Lieutenant General Lewis Burwell "Chesty" Puller of World War II and Korean War fame was one of his direct descendants. Burwell is buried at the Burwell Cemetery in Mecklenburg County, on land that was once part of the original Stoneland Plantation.

Chapter 3

COLONEL CHARLES DABNEY

(1745–1829)

Charles Dabney was born in 1745 on his family's estate, Aldingham, in Hanover County. He was a son of Anne Barret Dabney and Colonel William Dabney, who came from a long line of prominent local public officials. The Dabneys were originally Huguenot immigrants who arrived in Virginia in the 1650s. Like the sons of other affluent planters of the time, Dabney received a well-rounded education and also benefited from observing the leadership style of successful individuals who operated in his family's social circles. In 1775, he was appointed a captain in Patrick Henry's regiment of militiamen who were tasked with capturing a supply of powder that had been taken from Williamsburg by Royal Governor Lord Dunmore and his forces. From May to December 1776, Dabney then commanded a unit of Hanover and Louisa County minutemen known as Dabney's Legion. It was so named because it was larger than a company but not big enough to form a regiment. The group also contained a number of Dabney's relatives, including his brother George and his first cousin James, who were both captains. The legion was later incorporated into the Continental Line in December 1776 through the Third Virginia Regiment; Dabney was appointed to the rank of major. In that capacity, he possibly saw action at the Battle of Princeton. He was later appointed a lieutenant colonel in the Second Virginia Regiment on June 23, 1777. That October, he may have also fought at the Battle of Germantown. Following a winter stationed at Valley Forge, Dabney saw action at the Battle of Monmouth in Brigadier General William Smallwood's brigade and was then rendered supernumerary in September 1778. In January 1779, Dabney returned to the field as lieutenant colonel of the Second Virginia State Regiment and served under Major General Anthony Wayne at the Battle of Stony Point. In the midst of that engagement, Dabney and his legion assaulted a well-defended fortress in a fierce bayonet attack.

As commander of the Virginia State Regiment, Dabney continued to see action as the war shifted to Virginia, commanding all military posts below Williamsburg. Around this time, Governor Thomas Jefferson also tasked Dabney with assembling a team to, potentially, capture the newly minted British Brigadier General Benedict Arnold, who was operating in the area. However, substantial British reinforcements arrived, and the project never came to fruition. Lord Cornwallis and his army were raiding as far north as Petersburg, and General Washington ordered the Marquis de Lafayette to command a force, including Dabney's unit, to help repel the British threat. Thus, Dabney spent the summer months of 1781 on the move throughout central Virginia, skirmishing regularly with British forces. By August 29, 1781, Dabney had reported that he had approximately two hundred troops ready for service and was busy trying to secure clothes and arms to properly equip them. Following operations around Goochland County during that time, Dabney and his force began to move toward Yorktown in order to assist with the impending siege. Initially, Dabney's regiment was posted between Williamsburg and Yorktown with instructions to intercept all communication between the two locations. To Dabney's chagrin, he discovered that a seventeen-year-old cousin of his was acting as a courier for a group of Williamsburg ladies and transporting messages to British officers in Yorktown. Dabney was faced with the unpleasant duty of having to report the teenage boy as a spy to General Washington and was horrified when the commander in chief ordered the boy's execution. After further discussion, the punishment was reduced to thirty-nine lashes, which was supposed to be administered by Dabney himself. Deeply disturbed by the prospect of lashing a close relative, Dabney appealed for exemption from this duty. Finally, out

In 1775, Colonel Charles Dabney served as a captain in a militia regiment commanded by Patrick Henry (*shown here*). *New York Public Library.*

of consideration for Dabney, General Washington ordered the boy to be returned home to his mother with no punishment beyond the detention and fright he had already experienced.

Around October 6, General Washington assigned Dabney's regiment, along with some Delaware soldiers and Virginia militiamen, to General Knox to assist the American artillery. By October 10, 1781, Dabney had reported that his unit was helping draw their first parallel around Yorktown, at a distance of about five hundred yards, and American artillery were already in action against the British. Dabney hoped to be within two hundred yards of the British lines within the coming days. On October 16, his regiment, stationed at Battery 8B, was involved in helping repel a British attack on the Allied lines led by Lieutenant Colonel Robert Abercrombie. As part of a desperate effort to lengthen or even lift the siege, the British forces attacked the Allied position in hand-to-hand combat until they were repelled with the support of French reinforcements. The following day, Dabney was invited to General Washington's headquarters for dinner, and at this gathering, he was given a copy of the Articles of Capitulation. This was to inform Dabney of his duties for October 19 and would go on to become a cherished part of his personal papers.

After the British surrender at Yorktown, Dabney was promoted to colonel and given command of the American forces stationed at Portsmouth. In that capacity, he continued his efforts to recruit new troops and obtain equipment and supplies. In January 1782, state authorities gave him command of a state legion that was composed of the consolidated remnants of all Virginia state line units. This unit, tasked with protecting Virginia against any potential future British invasion, consisted of approximately 225 officers and men and was garrisoned in Richmond, Hampton and Yorktown. In this capacity, Dabney was stationed in Hampton, Virginia, and served there until shortly before the final ratification of peace in 1783. During that time, he was busy attending to administrative duties and lobbying efforts to help secure overdue pay for his men. He also tried to interest the Virginia state government in an invasion of Bermuda but to no avail. In addition, Dabney helped put down a small mutiny in September 1782. The legion was finally disbanded in April 1783, and Dabney received the thanks of Congress for his service. He was also an original member of the Society of the Cincinnati.

Following the war's conclusion, Dabney traveled to Kentucky to locate the lands to which he was entitled as compensation for his service. He explored the vast wilderness with only a blanket, a rifle and two hired men and, by all

Left: Colonel Charles Dabney saw action at the Battle of Germantown, serving in a brigade commanded by then Brigadier General William Smallwood (*shown here*). *New York Public Library.*

Right: Colonel Charles Dabney fought at the Battle of Stony Point, serving under Major General Anthony Wayne (*shown here*). *New York Public Library.*

accounts, enjoyed that period of relative solitude. One notable memory from the journey was seeing a herd of buffalo. Though Dabney did eventually secure valuable land, he figured there was little chance of his holding it as a nonresident, so he quickly sold the property and returned home. Thereafter, he spent several years lobbying the Virginia General Assembly to make payment to officers and soldiers for their wartime services. Dabney also quickly settled into life as a prominent Hanover County planter, operating a grain mill and serving as a copartner for a local blacksmith shop. When it came to the treatment of his slaves, he was considered a humane master given the context of the times. A nephew later remarked that he believed Dabney would have emancipated his slaves if he could have figured out a way for them to effectively subsist on their own and provide for themselves. Late in life, Dabney attempted to formulate a plan whereby he would bequeath the slaves to another nephew with an injunction to hire them out and pay the slaves a portion of the proceeds. While the plan did not come to fruition, it does demonstrate that Dabney was trying to support his slaves within the socioeconomic constraints of the era.

As Dabney approached his twilight years, he was considered an elder statesman in Hanover County and the surrounding areas. In 1800, he served as a presidential elector for the Commonwealth of Virginia. A lifelong bachelor, Dabney also enjoyed supporting his numerous nieces and nephews and visiting his brother and fellow veteran Captain George Dabney at his plantation, known as the Grove. He also continued his efforts to advocate for the proper compensation of Revolutionary War veterans, working with prominent figures like Chief Justice John Marshall. During this period, Dabney's friends, family and colleagues sought his guidance on a number of matters, such as when U.S. Attorney General William Wirt wrote to him in 1819 to discuss Major General Andrew Jackson's campaign against the Spanish in Florida. When the Marquis de Lafayette visited the United States in 1824, he sent his "affectionate regards" on learning that an elderly Dabney was too feeble to meet him in Richmond. Dabney passed away on December 15, 1829, and his estate was later determined to be worth $22,730.45—over $750,000 at modern rates when adjusted for inflation. It is believed that Dabney was buried on a corner of the Aldingham estate, though the exact location of his grave site has since been lost to time. Among his collateral descendants were several Confederate Army officers, including Major General J.E.B. Stuart and Major Robert Lewis Dabney, who served as chief of staff for Lieutenant General Thomas J. "Stonewall" Jackson.

In Colonel Charles Dabney's later life, a number of individuals sought his guidance, including U.S. Attorney General William Wirt (shown here). New York Public Library.

Chapter 4

LIEUTENANT COLONEL WILLIAM DARKE
(1736–1801)

One of the more colorful senior Virginia militia officers present during the Siege of Yorktown was Lieutenant Colonel William Darke. Known widely for his fiery temper and brash personality, Darke had an eventful military career that spanned multiple conflicts. Born in Philadelphia in 1736, he was a son of Joseph Darke and his wife, whose name is no longer known. Darke descended from Quaker settlers who had established themselves in Bucks County, Pennsylvania. He was also a cousin of Dr. Benjamin Rush, who would go on to become a signer of the Declaration of Independence. In 1740, Darke and his family moved to Shepherdstown, Virginia, which is now located in West Virginia's Jefferson County. Later, in 1755, he served in the Virginia militia during the French and Indian War. Tradition holds that Darke served under George Washington's command and saw action during Major General Edward Braddock's disastrous expedition to Fort Duquesne. However, modern historians question this claim, as primary source evidence to support it is lacking. Nevertheless, based on letters written by Darke, there is strong reason to believe that he had a long association with George Washington that predated the Revolutionary War.

In the mid-1760s, Darke married a widow named Sarah Deleyea, and he had at least three sons and one daughter with her. He also served as the guardian of an orphaned teenager named Thomas Worthington, who went on to serve as governor of Ohio from 1814 to 1818. Little else is known about Darke's life during the 1760s. However, as clouds of war approached in the mid-1770s, Darke promptly reentered the public arena as an ardent supporter of the patriot cause. Such sentiment was common among residents of the Upper Potomac region, who responded enthusiastically to calls for troops. In late 1775, Darke recruited a company of men that went on to become part of the Eighth Virginia Regiment, sometimes known as the German Regiment because of its strong contingent of German-speaking Shenandoah Valley settlers. At the time, the regiment was commanded by Colonel Peter Muhlenberg, who went on to become a major general in the Continental Army. Darke was commissioned a captain on February 9, 1776, and faced arduous service later that year as the regiment roamed from the Carolinas down to Florida under the command of Major General Charles Lee. During this period, Darke lost nearly half of his company to disease before returning north to the main army. He was also inexplicably passed over for a well-earned promotion, causing administrative controversy that had to ultimately be resolved by General Washington himself.

Darke was finally promoted to major retroactive to January 4, 1777, for purposes of seniority, but the promotion did not take effect until September that year. In the meantime, he spent the first half of 1777 on detached duty, working closely with then Brigadier General Anthony Wayne and Colonel Daniel Morgan. In this capacity, Darke commanded a company of 150 riflemen who harassed the British in New Jersey and participated in the Battle of Short Hills. Darke also served in a special light infantry unit, commanded by Brigadier General William Maxwell, that saw action at the Battle of Cooch's Bridge as well as at the Battle of Brandywine. However, while leading a forward detachment at the Battle of Germantown, Darke was captured, and he would go on to spend the next three years in captivity. He was initially imprisoned on a prison ship in New York and later sent to Long Island. While Darke was promoted to lieutenant colonel during this time, he later had to defend the promotion's validity since he had been unable to perform his duties while in captivity. Darke was finally released in October

Dr. Benjamin Rush (*shown here*), a signer of the Declaration of Independence, was a cousin of Lieutenant Colonel William Darke. *New York Public Library.*

Lieutenant Colonel William Darke.
Author's collection.

1780 in a prisoner exchange that included the British lieutenant governor of Quebec and the Crown's superintendent of Indian affairs, Lieutenant Colonel Henry Hamilton, who had been captured by Virginia state troops in February 1779.

Following his release, Darke returned home just as British forces were starting to commence military operations in Virginia. On December 30, 1780, newly minted British Brigadier General Benedict Arnold arrived in Virginia with over 1,800 troops, and he attacked the new state capital, Richmond, the following month. Then a larger British force under Lord Cornwallis moved into the area, prompting the Virginia General Assembly to flee to Charlottesville. In a frenzied attempt to respond, a largely inexperienced force of Virginia militia was defeated near Petersburg that April. Alarmed by this sequence of events, Governor Thomas Jefferson appealed to Brigadier General Daniel Morgan to raise an army in the Shenandoah Valley to help repel this British threat. Morgan quickly enlisted Darke's help, along with that of Horatio Gates, to recruit solders for this purpose. Shortly thereafter, Darke took command of a regiment of Frederick and Berkeley

County residents and marched with them toward Williamsburg. Arriving on July 7, 1781, shortly after the Battle of Green Spring, Darke and his force remained encamped in Williamsburg while Lord Cornwallis established his base at Yorktown. Following General Washington's arrival in Williamsburg on September 14, 1781, Darke committed the now legendary faux pas of approaching the commander in chief at an officers' reception without being officially summoned. While to many observers, this may have appeared to be an egregious breach of military protocol, it accurately reflected Darke's blunt, no-nonsense personality. Furthermore, he likely thought he did not need permission to greet an old friend whom he had known for many years. Darke may have also been eager to show gratitude for his freedom from British captivity, which General Washington had helped secure.

A few days later, Darke and his regiment marched toward Yorktown. Once there, they served on the siege lines outside of Yorktown in Brigadier General Edward Stevens's brigade. Although Darke was still technically a Continental Line officer, he remained active during the siege commanding his militia regiment, which occupied itself with digging entrenchments and dodging incoming British artillery. During this time, many under Darke's command contracted malaria and had to be sent home. Darke, however, persevered and was present to see the British surrender on October 19, 1781. Shortly thereafter, Darke's regiment helped escort British troops to captivity in Winchester.

Following the Yorktown campaign, Darke returned home to take his place as a prominent local military and civic leader. In 1785, he became an agent for the Potomac Company, a public works project led by General Washington that aimed to make the upper Potomac River more navigable, thus ensuring increased commercial river traffic. While that project ultimately proved unsuccessful, it provided Darke the opportunity to work closely with General Washington. Three years later, Darke was elected along with Major General Adam Stephen to serve as a delegate from Berkeley County to the Virginia Constitutional Convention. Both men voted to ratify the U.S. Constitution. It is also believed that Darke played a small role in General Washington's 1789 presidential inauguration, gifting Washington the sword he wore at his official swearing in. The following year, the pair met again in Shepherdstown as Washington sought Darke's guidance on where to place the new national capital.

In the spring of 1791, Darke was elected to represent Berkeley County in the Virginia House of Delegates. However, he never took his seat, because President Washington called him back to military service. Specifically, Darke

An undated note from Lieutenant Colonel William Darke to Major General Horatio Gates. *New York Public Library.*

was asked to help lead an expedition north of the Ohio River to combat Miami Indians who were attacking American settlers in the region. Under the overall command of Major General Arthur St. Clair, Darke led three battalions of Virginia, Maryland and frontier-based militiamen, which included his son Captain Joseph Darke, who served with the Virginians. The ill-equipped 1,400-man force, suffering from low morale, feuding officers and bad weather, was soundly defeated in a surprise attack at the Battle of the Wabash on November 4, 1791. In a few hours of fighting, over 900 Americans were reportedly killed. The survivors were able to retreat thanks to cover provided by Darke and his troops. However, he was seriously wounded in the process, and his son Joseph was killed. Despite this disastrous outcome, Darke was able to escape with his reputation intact, thanks to his efforts during the battle. In addition, he was careful to quickly report his version of events to President Washington, which involved critiques of St. Clair's leadership as well as accusations of cowardice leveled toward other officers. Darke later testified against St. Clair in Philadelphia and consulted with President Washington on which officers should potentially succeed him in leading future expeditions against the Native Americans.

In 1794, Darke took the field again to help put down the Whiskey Rebellion. The Virginia General Assembly appointed him a brigadier general, and he led

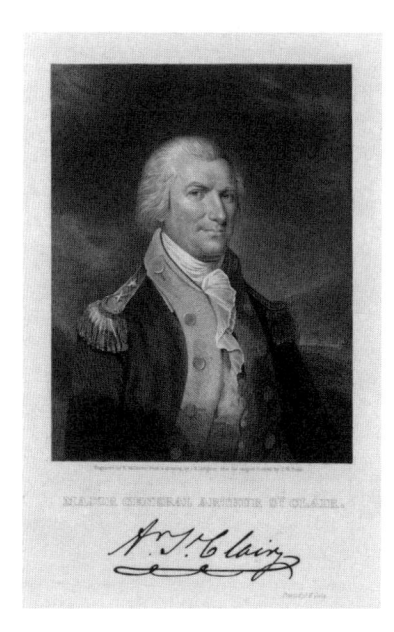

Lieutenant Colonel William Darke served under Major General Arthur St. Clair (*shown here*) at the disastrous Battle of the Wabash in 1791. *New York Public Library.*

troops to support that campaign at least as far north as Cumberland, Maryland, where they were reviewed by President Washington. This was likely the last time Darke saw the commander in chief. In 1800, Darke supported Thomas Jefferson for president, and he later offered advice on appointments to Jefferson as well as to James Madison. He last held public office as a member of the court for Jefferson County, which had split off from Berkeley County. However, it is unclear whether he actually attended the first meeting of that body on November 10, 1801. Darke passed away in Shepherdstown on November 26, 1801, and was buried at the nearby Engle Cemetery. To honor this distinguished Revolutionary War veteran, Darkesville in West Virginia and Darke County in Ohio are both named after him.

Chapter 5

COLONEL ELIAS EDMONDS JR.
(1756–1800)

Elias Edmonds Jr. was one of the few senior Virginia militia officers at Yorktown who had spent much of his prior wartime service as an artillery commander. A son of Elias Edmonds Sr. and his wife, Elizabeth (Miller), Edmonds was born in 1756 in Fauquier County. The Edmonds clan originally hailed from Lancaster County, Virginia, but Elias Edmonds Sr. moved to Fauquier County around 1741. There, he established the Edmonium estate, which was situated a few miles northwest of Warrenton. Elias Edmonds Sr. later became a prosperous tobacco farmer and served as a colonial magistrate and militia captain during the French and Indian War. Following a childhood spent at Edmonium, Elias Edmonds Jr. served as a clerk for Phillip Lee, a prominent Dumfries merchant. However, after the outbreak of war, he quickly joined the revolutionary cause and was elected a lieutenant in a regiment called the Culpeper Minutemen, who were among the first minutemen raised in Virginia. This unit, commanded by Colonel Lawrence Taliaferro and Major Thomas Marshall (father of future U.S. Supreme Court Chief Justice John Marshall), consisted of 150 men from Culpeper County, 100 from Orange County and another 100 from Fauquier. Thus, Edmonds and John Marshall served as young lieutenants together in this regiment, which was well known for its white banner depicting a rattlesnake and bearing phrases such as "Don't Tread on Me" and "Liberty or Death." Wearing green hunting shirts and armed with hunting rifles, knives and tomahawks, the Culpeper Minutemen saw action at the Battle of Great Bridge in December 1775.

Colonel Elias Edmonds Jr. first served under the father of future U.S. Supreme Court Chief Justice John Marshall (*shown here*). *New York Public Library.*

Following the disbandment of the Culpeper Minutemen in January 1776, Edmonds transferred over to Colonel Thomas Marshall's new unit, the Third Virginia Regiment, and went on to see action during the New York Campaign and at the Battles of Trenton and Princeton. In 1777, he was promoted to captain and commanded a company in the Virginia State Artillery Regiment. Shortly thereafter, he was ordered south, and he participated in the Continental Army's campaigns in North and South Carolina, seeing action at the Battle of Camden, among other places. During this time, Edmonds was also promoted to lieutenant colonel and exercised regimental-level artillery command. In 1781, he returned to Virginia and assumed command as a full colonel of the Fauquier County militia.

In that capacity, he marched his troops to Yorktown and took part in the siege, serving in Brigadier General Edward Stevens's brigade. Following Cornwallis's surrender, Edmonds continued his military service until the close of the war. After returning to Edmonium, he married his first cousin Frances Edmonds on January 11, 1786, with whom he would have three children. His daughter Octavia would go on to marry a son of Colonel William Grayson, a Continental Army commander who later served as one of Virginia's U.S. senators. In 1786, Edmonds was also elected to the Virginia House of Delegates and won reelection two additional times. He once again represented Fauquier County in the House of Delegates in 1791 before passing away in 1800 at the age of forty-four.

Chapter 6

LIEUTENANT COLONEL WILLIAM FONTAINE (1754–1810)

William Fontaine was born on January 22, 1754, in Lunenburg County, a son of Colonel Peter Fontaine Jr. and Elizabeth (Winston) Fontaine. The family moved to Halifax County a year later. In 1759, they moved again to the northwestern Beaverdam section of Hanover County, where they established their home, known as Rock Castle. Fontaine enrolled at The College of William & Mary in 1772, completing a year or two of education there before returning to Hanover County to be taught by tutors. An ardent patriot, Fontaine raised a company of troops from the Amherst County area at the commencement of the war. In September 1775, he was commissioned a captain in the Second Virginia Regiment, serving in that capacity until March 1776. During that period, Fontaine saw action at the Battle of Great Bridge on December 9, 1775. He was later appointed a captain in the Hanover County militia, in which he was active throughout 1777 and 1778. This included a brief period of service with General Washington's main army near Philadelphia as well as White Plains, New York, as a member of a volunteer troop formation raised by Thomas Nelson. In December 1778, Fontaine was appointed a major in the Virginia Convention Guard, which was tasked with guarding the British and Hessian troops who composed the Convention Army that surrendered following the Battle of Saratoga. It was based in the Charlottesville area in the Albemarle Barracks. Fontaine was promoted to lieutenant colonel in March 1779 and served in this capacity until May 1781, when the regiment was disbanded. Nevertheless, Fontaine remained an active militia leader and saw service during Benedict Arnold's

Lieutenant Colonel William Fontaine was among those assigned to guard the Convention Army, which had been captured at the Battle of Saratoga. *New York Public Library.*

invasion of Virginia in late 1780 and early 1781. Later that year, he raised a formation of troops and marched to Yorktown, where he served during the siege. By all accounts, Fontaine was considered a meritorious officer who was highly respected by the men serving under his command.

Following the war, Fontaine returned to Hanover County and spent the 1780s buying out his siblings' interests in Rock Castle, where he would live for the remainder of his life. Active in county politics, he was involved in a duel with William Macon in 1788 over an election dispute. In 1789, he married Ann Morris, with whom he would go on to have nine children. An active planter, Fontaine was also fond of breeding merino sheep, sharing that interest with his friend Thomas Jefferson. Fontaine also engaged in land speculation during this period, doing business in other Virginia counties as well as in North and South Carolina. Continuing his civic and military duties, he also spent the postwar years serving as a justice of the peace and a colonel in the Hanover County militia. Fontaine passed away on October 6, 1810, and was buried in Beaverdam Cemetery in Hanover County. His wife was awarded a Revolutionary War widow's pension in 1838; she passed away in 1852.

Chapter 7

COLONEL WILLIAM GRIFFIN
(1742–1793)

William Griffin was born on January 29, 1742, in Richmond County. Descending from a prominent Tidewater family, he was a son of Richmond County Sheriff Leroy Griffin and his wife, Mary Anne Bertrand. He was also a grandson of House of Burgesses member Thomas Griffin of Richmond County. After receiving a private education befitting his societal station, Griffin established himself in King and Queen County, where he was a landowner and a local church vestry member. He married Susanna Chiswell, a daughter of Colonel John Chiswell, in 1771 and had at least two children with her. Susanna had been previously married to House of Burgesses Speaker John Robinson, who passed away in 1766. They made their home at their family estate, known as Clifton, which was located along the Mattaponi River. In October 1772, Griffin was appointed as a justice to the King and Queen County Court. A short time later, as the clouds of war approached, Griffin and several of his brothers became devoted patriots and contributed significantly to the revolutionary cause.

Griffin's older brother, Dr. Corbin Griffin of Yorktown, served as a Continental Army surgeon and was a state senator during the war's later stages. Another brother, Colonel Samuel Griffin, also served in the Continental Army as an aide to Major General Charles Lee. Wounded at the Battle of Harlem Heights, he later played a pivotal role in the lead-up to the Battle of Trenton by helping draw Hessian reinforcements commanded by Colonel Carl von Donop away from General Washington's main army.

Forced to retire from the army due to ill health, Samuel Griffin served as mayor of Williamsburg and was later a state legislator as well as a member of the U.S. House of Representatives. Meanwhile, a third brother named Cyrus Griffin served as a wartime Virginia legislator as well as the eighth president of the Congress of the Confederation in 1788. While his brothers performed these important military and political services, William Griffin was an active patriot leader in King and Queen County. He commanded the local militia with the rank of colonel and also served as sheriff. During the Siege of Yorktown, he quickly advanced his King and Queen County forces to Gloucester Point, where he went on to command one of the primary regiments in Brigadier General George Weedon's brigade. Following the war, Griffin returned to King and Queen County, where he passed away on February 11, 1793, at the age of fifty-one. His beloved home, Clifton, burned down in subsequent years, though it was later rebuilt in the nineteenth century before falling again into disrepair. Some of its ruins are still in existence.

Cyrus Griffin served as the eighth president of the Congress of the Confederation in 1788. *New York Public Library.*

Chapter 8

COLONEL JAMES INNES

(1754–1798)

One of Tidewater Virginia's most distinguished Revolutionary War leaders was Colonel James Innes, who saw significant action as a Continental Army officer and a Virginia militia commander. Born in 1754 in Caroline County, Innes was the son of the Reverend Robert Innes and Catherine Richards. The Reverend Robert Innes was a graduate of King's College who, after immigrating to Virginia from Scotland, took the position of rector of Drysdale Parish in Caroline County. The younger Innes therefore grew up on a small farm about twenty miles southwest of Tappahannock, where he received his primary education from noted area educator Donald Robertson. Following his father's death in 1765, Innes became the ward of prominent lawyer and legislator Edmund Pendleton, who was the executor of his father's estate. In 1770, he began his studies at The College of William & Mary, where he read law under George Wythe. Innes was also active in the Flat Hat Club, which was an early College fraternity. He graduated in 1773 and remained at the College, serving as the head usher of the Grammar School. Furthermore, he played an integral role in organizing local patriot militia forces in 1775. As a commander of the Williamsburg Volunteer Company, which was composed mostly of William & Mary students, Innes rallied his forces to secure military stores that were being targeted for confiscation by Lord Dunmore and his British forces. These actions prompted Innes to be expelled from the College by its loyalist faculty.

Following his departure from William & Mary, Innes immediately engaged in military service. In February 1776, he was elected captain of an artillery company in the Virginia militia, and he was active in helping expel Lord Dunmore and his forces from Virginia. That November, Innes was appointed a lieutenant colonel in the Fifteenth Virginia Regiment and saw action at the Battles of Trenton and Princeton. Following the latter engagement, he had the somber duty of traveling to Fredericksburg to convey the news of Brigadier General Hugh Mercer's death to community leaders. A few months later, Innes served valiantly during the Battles of Brandywine and Germantown and was commended for rallying his troops. Later in 1777, Innes served briefly in the Sixth Virginia Regiment before going home on recruiting duty in early 1778. In that capacity, he also served as a special messenger for General Washington to Patrick Henry, conveying to the Virginia governor the latest information about the Virginia Continental Line. This could be the factual foundation for the popular legend that Innes served as one of General Washington's wartime aides. Innes did not end up returning to Continental Army service, having grown frustrated with military politics and desiring a return to a civilian way of life. He resigned his commission on June 12, 1778.

Around this time, Innes married Elizabeth "Betsy" Cocke of Williamsburg, and he would go on to have two children with her. He had been a longtime suitor of Betsy's, and one of his professed frustrations with Continental Line service was that it had postponed his long-awaited marriage to her. Innes also continued his reorientation toward state-level administrative and political service, accepting appointment as a commissioner to the Virginia Navy Board in October 1778. Shortly thereafter, he served as president of the Board of War, overseeing the affairs of all Continental Army and militia troops in the state, with a special focus on recruiting and training. This work became progressively more difficult as new recruits proved harder and harder to find and equip, especially following the American surrender at Charleston in May 1780, which wiped out much of the Virginia Continental

As a young William & Mary student, Colonel James Innes read law under George Wythe (*shown here*). *New York Public Library.*

Line. As the war progressed, Innes also served in the Virginia House of Delegates from 1780 to 1781, where he represented James City County and, later, Williamsburg.

During Benedict Arnold's invasion of Virginia in early 1781, Innes took again to the field, serving as second in command of local militia forces under Thomas Nelson. In this capacity, he was credited with helping prevent a British amphibious landing at Jamestown. However, Innes also faced difficulties during this time as he had a tense relationship with Baron von Steuben, who commanded all American forces in Virginia. As spring approached, Innes took command of the militia forces assembling in the Gloucester area, right across the York River from Yorktown. He spent the next few months shadowing British forces under Generals William Phillips and Charles Cornwallis as they operated across central and eastern Virginia. While Cornwallis and his troops began their trek toward Yorktown, Innes and his forces repositioned themselves in Gloucester. As the Siege of Yorktown commenced, Innes was replaced in command by Brigadier General George Weedon. Innes had been Governor Thomas Nelson's preferred choice for commander, but a letter from the Marquis de Lafayette in support of Weedon helped secure Weedon the position. However, Innes continued to serve in the area as a senior officer and commanded one of Weedon's main regiments. Then, in a reorganization on September 27, 1781, Weedon gave Innes command of an advance brigade consisting of three battalions of infantry, one of grenadiers and a small formation of cavalry led by Lieutenant Colonel John Webb. Shortly thereafter, Weedon utilized this force to engage in foraging expeditions near the British lines at Gloucester Point. Thus, Innes and his troops proved integral in helping contain Lieutenant Colonel Banastre Tarleton and his forces.

Following the war, Innes began to transition toward a legal career and quickly became one of Virginia's most prominent and successful attorneys. There are no surviving records of his professional training in this area, but it appears that he was performing legal work as early as 1780. Stating a desire to pursue work in civilian law, he turned down an opportunity to become the Continental Army's judge advocate general in July 1782. Instead of riding the traditional rural legal circuit, Innes based himself in Richmond, where he could focus on practicing before the state's top courts. Considering his standing in the state's legal community, it is no surprise that the General Assembly elected him attorney general of Virginia in 1786. He would go on to serve in that role for nearly a decade. In June 1788, Innes also served as Williamsburg's lone delegate to the Virginia Convention that ratified the U.S. Constitution. In that capacity, he was a strong supporter of ratification and was even commended by anti-ratification advocate Patrick Henry for his elegant and persuasive oratory.

In subsequent years, Innes politely declined multiple calls to pursue federal office, turning down offers to potentially serve in Congress, the Supreme Court and as U.S. attorney general. These refusals stemmed in part from Innes's preference for serving in local and state-level capacities. However, his failing health was also a critical factor, owing largely to his enormous weight. Often labeled one of the largest men in the state, Innes could not ride a normal horse or sit in a normal chair. He also struggled with recurring fevers and bouts of pain that dated to at least 1782. Nevertheless, Innes did accept two lower-level diplomatic appointments during the Washington administration. In 1794, he served as a presidential agent to the people of Kentucky to convey details about the U.S government's impending treaty with Spain concerning free navigation of the Mississippi River. Then, in 1796, Innes was appointed to serve as a commissioner to examine the details of damages awarded to U.S. citizens under Article 6 of the Jay Treaty. While serving in this capacity, Innes passed away in Philadelphia on August 2, 1798, at the age of forty-four. He was buried in Christ Church Burial Ground near Benjamin Franklin's tomb. His brother Harry Innes also had a distinguished legal career and was instrumental in establishing Kentucky as an independent state.

A miniature painting of Colonel James Innes by Charles Willson Peale. *Virginia Museum of History & Culture (1993.113.1-2).*

Chapter 9

BRIGADIER GENERAL ROBERT LAWSON
(1748–1805)

One of the more elusive Virginia militia leaders who served at Yorktown was Brigadier General Robert Lawson. Despite his distinguished career as a soldier and public servant, much of his life is shrouded in mystery. For instance, relatively little is known about his childhood. Lawson was likely born in 1748 in Prince George County, though some sources claim that he was born in Yorkshire, England, and immigrated to Virginia with his parents, Benjamin Lawson and Elizabeth Claiborne. However, some of his descendants have disputed that assertion. Lawson did not enter the public record until approximately 1769, when he married Sarah Meriwether Pierce, with whom he would go on to have five children. In the early 1770s, he emerged in southside Virginia as an active lawyer, planter and businessman. While it is beyond dispute that Lawson practiced law, it is unknown whether he underwent any sort of qualifying process for that profession. In June 1775, he was elected to the Prince Edward County Committee of Safety, and he later served on its state-level equivalent. Then, on January 12, 1776, Lawson became a major in the Fourth Virginia Regiment, where he was active in helping repel Lord Dunmore and his forces from the state. That August, he was promoted to lieutenant colonel as his regiment went north to join General Washington's main army, where it later saw action at the Battles of Trenton and Princeton. However, it appears that Lawson himself spent most of this time back in Virginia attending to recruiting duties.

Frustrated by not being in the field, Lawson attempted to resign his commission. However, when no action was taken on the request, he rejoined

A painting by John Trumbull depicting the death of Brigadier General Hugh Mercer at the Battle of Princeton. *New York Public Library.*

his regiment in New Jersey in August 1777, serving as acting commander. A few days later, he was promoted to colonel and regimental commander. Though details are scarce, it is likely that he served at the Battles of Brandywine and Germantown. In the weeks following Germantown, Lawson was among a group of officers who lobbied for Continental Army reform, citing, among other things, inadequate pay and unfair practices concerning promotion of officers. Shortly thereafter, he again stated his intention to resign. This time, Congress granted the request, which was effective as of December 17, 1777. Back in Virginia at his plantation, Rosedale, located near modern-day Farmville, Lawson immersed himself in political activities, winning election to the Virginia House of Delegates in 1778. The following year, he also served on the state's Board of War. However, as the war began to shift southward, Lawson once again took to the field as a military commander. First, he was appointed a brigadier general of militia to help repel the Collier-Mathews Raid in May 1779. In that capacity, he played in integral role in protecting Smithfield from British attack.

In October 1780, Lawson was also active in resisting a British incursion up the James River, commanded by then Brigadier General Alexander Leslie. Leading over eight hundred militia volunteers, he helped support Major General Peter Muhlenberg's efforts to, eventually, keep the British forces contained to the Portsmouth area. For this service, Lawson received a resolution of thanks from the General Assembly. Then, in early 1781, Lawson was back in the field for a third time in response to Benedict Arnold's rapid amphibious raid into central Virginia. Following the initial incursion, he once again found himself commanding troops in a virtual stalemate against entrenched British forces based in Portsmouth. This relative inactivity was unsettling to Lawson, and he longed to be in the thick of the action with Major General Nathanael Greene's forces in the Carolinas. Greene, in turn, was an admirer of Lawson's leadership skills and was certainly open to the idea of Lawson joining his force. Governor Thomas Jefferson later approved this proposal, and Lawson and his command were en route to join Greene's force by March 1781.

Along with thousands of other Virginia and North Carolina militia, they arrived in time to participate in the Battle of Guilford Courthouse. Stationed behind North Carolina militia that was flanked by Continental regulars, Lawson's brigade formed a second line of Greene's force along with a brigade of Virginia militia commanded by Brigadier General Edward Stevens. In the midst of a heavy attack from the British, Lawson and his forces held their ground, earning high praise from observers. They were forced to pull back only when faced with superior British numbers as well as the wounding of Lawson's fellow brigade commander, Brigadier General Edward Stevens.

Following the battle, Lawson returned home with the intention of rejoining Greene near Salisbury, North Carolina, to lead a new militia force. However, by mid-May 1781, Cornwallis's Army had entered Virginia, reaching as far north as Petersburg. Governor Jefferson therefore redirected Lawson to assume command of all Virginia militia forces south of the Appomattox River. Around this time, Lawson also joined forces with the Marquis de Lafayette's small army, operating in and around central Virginia through the summer months. When he was not in the field, he played a vital role in organizing and equipping militia forces from across the state. During the Siege of Yorktown, Lawson commanded a militia brigade stationed along the siege lines with Stevens's brigade. Unlike their counterparts in Gloucester, Lawson's troops saw little to no combat. However, following the British surrender, they were charged with escorting the new prisoners of war to internment camps farther north in Virginia and Maryland. In total, Lawson oversaw the movement of a three-mile-long procession of over six thousand British and Hessian troops. Following this mission, potential orders to rejoin General Greene in the Carolinas never materialized, so Lawson resumed his public service activities.

Between 1782 and 1783, he served on the Council of State and rejoined the Virginia House of Delegates. In 1783, Lawson was instrumental in helping establish Hampden-Sydney College, and he served on its board of trustees for the rest of his life. In addition, he was an active member of the Society of the Cincinnati. As the 1780s progressed, Lawson continued in his public duties, serving as deputy attorney general and as county lieutenant for Prince Edward County. His most notable work during this time was arguably his service as a representative for Prince Edward County during the Virginia Convention for ratification of the U.S. Constitution in June 1788. Along with Patrick Henry, Richard Henry Lee, George Mason and others, Lawson formed a powerful Anti-Federalist bloc that argued against ratification, citing concerns about the potentially enormous power of a central government.

Considering the distinguished array of public service and military roles that Lawson played in the 1770s and 1780s, it is perplexing that the details of his life beyond 1789 are murky at best. It appears that he and his family moved that year to Lexington, Kentucky, and as the 1790s wore on, he exchanged correspondence with wartime colleagues such as Major General Adam Stephen and Thomas Jefferson. However, struggles with alcoholism and family conflict appear to have facilitated his return to Virginia in 1797, where he spent most of his time in his native Prince Edward County. During his final years, Lawson was reportedly a destitute invalid, living under the care of fellow Society of the Cincinnati members in Richmond. He died there on March 28, 1805, and was buried at St. John's Episcopal Church following an official funeral at the state capitol. At least three of his children continued living in Kentucky or elsewhere beyond Virginia. His son Columbus Lawson was killed at the Battle of New Orleans in 1815, while his daughter America Lawson went on to marry a Louisiana Territory judge. Another son, Jeremiah Lawson, became a noted Methodist minister in Kentucky,

In 1788, Brigadier General Robert Lawson worked with George Mason (*shown here*) and others to oppose ratification of the U.S. Constitution. *New York Public Library.*

Ohio and Missouri. Ultimately, despite the troubled final chapter of his life, Lawson was held in high regard by many of his friends and colleagues, who described him as a worthy officer and public servant.

Chapter 10

COLONEL WILLIAM LEWIS
(UNCERTAIN)

The historical record clearly states that there was a Colonel William Lewis who commanded a contingent of Shenandoah Valley riflemen during the Siege of Yorktown. Prior to the siege, this unit had even been selected to accompany then Brigadier General Peter Muhlenberg's forces in September 1781 as they marched toward Yorktown. However, what is less clear is the specific identity of William Lewis, as there were several individuals who bore that name in Virginia during this period. Sadly, it appears that the Revolutionary War service of at least three of them has been mixed in the historical record over the generations, making it nearly impossible to determine which William Lewis commanded riflemen at Yorktown. Luckily, one traditional candidate can now be ruled out. A Major William Lewis of Loudoun County (who died in 1811) was once thought by some to be the individual who served at Yorktown. He rose in rank from first lieutenant to major in various Virginia Continental Line regiments and also served as brigade inspector of General Muhlenberg's brigade in 1778. However, other historians have questioned this claim of service at Yorktown, arguing that he was not from the Shenandoah Valley like the William Lewis of Yorktown fame. Moreover, Major William Lewis was captured at the fall of Charleston in 1780 and was held as a prisoner for the balance of the war. This makes it highly unlikely that he could have commanded militia forces at Yorktown. In recent years, this conclusion has been supported by DNA testing, which proved that Major William Lewis of Loudoun County was not related to the Lewis clan of the Shenandoah Valley.

The Colonel William Lewis present at Yorktown may have been a brother or nephew of Brigadier General Andrew Lewis *(depicted here)*. *New York Public Library.*

This leaves two leading candidates, William L. Lewis (1724–1811) of Augusta County and his son William J. Lewis (1766–1828) of Campbell County. The elder William Lewis was born in Ireland and was among Augusta County's earliest settlers. A son of John Lewis and Margaret (Lynn), he was also a brother of Andrew Lewis, who would go on to serve as a brigadier general in the Continental Army. According to some sources, William L. Lewis studied medicine in Philadelphia in the early 1750s and then returned to Staunton, Virginia, to practice medicine and manage his father's properties. In 1754, he married Ann Montgomery, with whom he would have eight children. The next year, he was supposedly wounded during Major General Edward Braddock's disastrous defeat during the French and Indian War. However, owing to a lack of substantiating sources, many historians have disputed this claim. By all accounts, William L. Lewis was a devoted patriot and quite possibly commanded Augusta County militia forces as a colonel during various phases of the Revolutionary War. One of his sons, Major John Lewis (1758–1823), served in the Ninth Virginia Regiment, was encamped at Valley Forge and later saw action at the Battle of Monmouth. In 1790, William L. Lewis moved to Sweet Spring, Virginia, where he died in 1811.

Meanwhile, his son William J. Lewis pursued a career in public service, serving in various state and federal elected offices. Interestingly, he used the middle initial *I* in his early years and then the middle initial *J* in his later life. Establishing himself at his plantation, Mount Athos, near Lynchburg, Virginia, he married Elizabeth Cabell and served several terms in the Virginia House of Delegates, where he was considered a respected leader. In 1816, he was elected to the U.S. House of Representatives, where he served a single term from 1817 to 1819. In October 1824, William J. Lewis had the distinction of meeting the Marquis de Lafayette during Lafayette's visit to Yorktown. For the occasion, Lewis wore traditional mountain dress and prided himself on representing the valiant men of the Shenandoah Valley. For this reason, many published sources maintain that it was William J. Lewis who commanded militia forces at Yorktown—and that could certainly be the case. However, it also seems somewhat unusual that a fifteen-year-old would have served as a militia colonel commanding a force of riflemen. As such, it cannot be dismissed that the actual Colonel William Lewis who served at Yorktown may have been his father. Further research will be required to sort out this interesting historical mystery.

In October 1824, the Marquis de Lafayette (*shown here*) met with Colonel William Lewis at Yorktown. *New York Public Library.*

Chapter 11

COLONEL REUBEN LINDSAY

(1747–1831)

Reuben Lindsay was born on January 15, 1747, in either Caroline County or Westmoreland County. He was a son of James and Sarah (Daniel) Lindsay, planters who originally resided near Port Royal. Around 1775, Lindsay moved to Albemarle County, purchasing approximately 750 acres of land on the east side of the Southwest Mountain. Lindsay quickly prospered as a successful tobacco merchant and was also known to be a devoted patriot. He reportedly advanced £1,000 in gold to help support the revolutionary cause, for which he was never reimbursed. In 1778, he married Sarah Walker, who was a daughter of noted King and Queen County–born explorer and physician Dr. Thomas Walker Jr. Moreover, Sarah Walker's brother, Colonel John Walker, served as an aide-de-camp to General Washington in the Continental Army. In the early days of the Revolutionary War, Lindsay commenced service as an officer in the Albemarle County militia. During this period, then Governor Thomas Jefferson offered Lindsay the post of county lieutenant; Lindsay reportedly declined the honor. However, he may have served in the post during the war's later stages. By early 1781, Lindsay was a colonel in the Albemarle County militia, and he was active in contesting Benedict Arnold's invasion of Virginia. He went on to command a militia regiment at the Siege of Yorktown.

Following the war, Lindsay returned to Albemarle County, where he served as a county magistrate. After his first wife's passing, he married Hannah Tidwell in 1789, with whom he had three daughters. Around this

Colonel Reuben Lindsay. *National Portrait Gallery.*

time, Lindsay decided that his new family needed a larger home, so he purchased several land tracts in modern-day Orange County and built a new home, known as Springfield. By 1796, Lindsay's Springfield Farm plantation consisted of more than two thousand acres, and by 1806, he owned twenty-eight enslaved persons, fifteen horses, a stage wagon and one riding carriage. In later years, he continued to enjoy a close friendship with Thomas Jefferson, who would often visit Springfield. Accordingly, Lindsay appears frequently in Jefferson's memorandum books between 1772 and 1823. He was also in regular contact with James Madison, who was a fellow Orange County resident. Lindsay never claimed bounty lands to which he was entitled, supposedly asserting that the freedom of his country was sufficient reward for his sacrifices. Lindsay passed away on September 22, 1831, and was buried in the Lindsay Family Cemetery in Gordonsville, Virginia. One of his sons-in-law, William F. Gordon, was a major general in the Virginia militia as well as a U.S. congressman between 1830 and 1835. Gordon was also integral in helping establish the University of Virginia.

Chapter 12

COLONEL SAMPSON MATHEWS
(CIRCA 1737–1807)

Colonel Sampson Mathews was the scion of a prominent Shenandoah Valley family who contributed significantly to the revolutionary cause. Born circa 1737, he was a son of John and Ann Archer Mathews, who were among the first European settlers to inhabit Augusta County. It is unclear whether John Mathews was of Scotch-Irish, Irish or Welsh origin; what is known is that he was a prominent local civic and religious leader who also served as a militia captain. Sampson Mathews was the eldest of ten siblings; two of his brothers, George and Archer, would also go on to pursue active public service careers. Sampson, educated at the Augusta Academy, was elected a captain of the Augusta County militia in 1755 at the outbreak of the French and Indian War. In that capacity, he served under Major General Edward Braddock alongside George Washington during the ill-fated Braddock Expedition. Mathews's father and several of his brothers also served during this campaign. Following his return home, Mathews was elected Augusta County sheriff in 1756 and was also active in the local Anglican church. In 1759, he married Mary Lockhart, with whom he would have four children: two sons and two daughters.

The early 1760s brought Mathews commercial success as he entered the mercantile business with his brother George. They began by operating a store in Staunton, Virginia, at the corner of Beverley and Augusta Streets, and they sometimes acted as land agents as well. Rapid success allowed them to spread their business interests to outposts throughout the region,

As a young captain, Colonel Sampson Mathews took part in Major General Edward Braddock's ill-fated expedition in 1755. *Library of Congress.*

including a second store in the Greenbrier district of western Virginia. The Mathews firm offered everything ranging from home goods to contracts for indentured servants and, sometimes, even enslaved persons. Furthermore, it grew to encompass an expansive Atlantic trade network. By the mid-1760s, Mathews was also operating a successful tavern in Staunton, and he served in important community leadership positions such as justice of the peace and vestryman at his local church. A few years later, he was integral in helping organize a new academy in Lexington, Virginia, that by 1773 was known as Liberty Hall. This institution would later evolve into what is now Washington and Lee University; Mathews served as one of its original trustees. The following year, he served as the chief procurement officer for an expedition led by Brigadier General Andrew Lewis against the Shawnee and Mingo Indians. Royal Governor Lord Dunmore tasked this force with pacifying Indian raids against White settlers in the region. Organizing at Mathews's tavern, Lewis and his troops launched a successful campaign that culminated in the Battle of Point Pleasant on October 10, 1774. Mathews himself was actively engaged in the campaign and, according to some sources, directly contributed to Shawnee Chief Cornstalk's retreat at the height of the battle.

With relations between the Americans and the British quickly souring, Sampson became an active patriot leader, serving on the Augusta County Committee of Safety in early 1775. Shortly thereafter, he met with representatives from neighboring counties to begin organizing militia units. George Mathews was given command of one of those companies, while Sampson Mathews went on to serve in the inaugural Virginia State Senate in 1776, which replaced the colonial-era Governor's Council. As a state senator, Mathews was initially active in efforts to expand the Continental Navy's Virginia fleet, helping superintend a factory in Staunton that made sail materials out of flax grown by area farmers. However, in the fall of 1777, a dispute with the Shawnee Indians stemming from the unwarranted execution of Chief Cornstalk by Virginia militia forces required Mathews to serve as a commissioner to help resolve the situation. Meanwhile, George Mathews had pursued service in the Continental Army, rising to the rank of colonel and serving as commander of the Ninth Virginia Regiment. However, he was captured along with the rest of his regiment at the Battle of Germantown, and they spent the next four years as prisoners of war.

In May 1778, Sampson Mathews was appointed a lieutenant colonel in the Augusta County militia, effectively holding a field commission of full colonel. This reflected his status as one of the county's most prominent leaders. He spent the next several months leading expeditions to root out reported Indian threats but saw no substantive action. By October 1780, Mathews had requested leave from the Virginia Senate to focus on his military duties. This was a wise move, as the center of the fighting would soon shift to Virginia. On January 1, 1781, Benedict Arnold launched a surprise invasion and moved up the James River toward Richmond with little resistance. Governor Thomas Jefferson had to flee the capital and subsequently called out the militia to help repel the British threat. Mathews, commanding forces from Augusta and Rockingham Counties, was directed to report to Brigadier General George Weedon in Fredericksburg and proceeded there with his 250 men on January 13, 1781. Having made the march from Staunton to Fredericksburg in four days, Mathews was ordered by General Muhlenberg to proceed thirty miles south to Bowling Green. Shortly thereafter, he was ordered to move toward Smithfield, Virginia, which was another eighty miles southeast. Throughout this period, Mathews lobbied for desperately needed supplies and provisions, citing problems with mutinous morale and exposure to the cold weather. By February 15, General Arnold's forces were pinned down in Portsmouth, Virginia, and Mathews and his troops were stationed there at an advanced outpost. However, by mid-April, they had returned to Staunton.

Following the Virginia General Assembly's evacuation from Richmond, it met at Trinity Episcopal Church in Staunton in June 1781. On June 12, it elected Thomas Nelson Jr. governor of Virginia, and Mathews administered the oath of office on June 19 in his capacity as an Augusta County justice of the peace. Immediately after, Mathews organized a regiment and headed to eastern Virginia, where he saw action on July 6, 1781, at the Battle of Green Spring outside of Williamsburg. On August 8, Mathews and his regiment went to Yorktown, where they were later assigned to Brigadier General Robert Lawson's brigade.

Colonel Sampson Mathews was called to help oppose the Virginia invasion of British Brigadier General Benedict Arnold (*shown here*) in January 1781. *New York Public Library.*

Following the British surrender, Mathews returned home and resumed his duties in the Virginia Senate. He later stepped down from his post as lieutenant colonel of the Augusta County militia on November 18, 1783. In the years that followed, Mathews continued to carry out his political and civic duties, serving a final term in the Virginia Senate in 1790 and as a justice of the peace and sheriff for Bath County following its creation in 1791. He resided in Bath County for the next decade, living at his estate, called Cloverdale.

Meanwhile, his brother George Mathews also followed a postwar career in public service. Following his release from British captivity, he was brevetted a brigadier general, and he was an original member of the Society of the Cincinnati. After the war, George Mathews moved to Georgia, where he went on to serve as that state's governor from 1787 to 1788 and again from 1793 to 1796. In between those terms, he represented Georgia's Third Congressional District in the U.S. House of Representatives from 1789 through 1791.

Sampson Mathews spent his final years living in a log house in Staunton with his second wife, Mary, whom he had married after his first wife's death. He passed away there on January 20, 1807. Mathews's family continued his public service tradition well into the nineteenth century. His son Sampson Mathews II went on to represent Bath County in the Virginia House of Delegates from 1809 to 1810. Meanwhile, his son-in-law, Lieutenant Colonel Thomas Posey, served as lieutenant governor of Kentucky from 1806 to 1808, as a U.S. senator for Louisiana from 1812 to 1813 and as governor of Indiana Territory from 1813 to 1816. Sampson Mathews's place of burial is unknown.

Chapter 13

LIEUTENANT COLONEL THOMAS MATHEWS (1742-1812)

Thomas Mathews was born in 1742 on the island of St. Kitts in the British West Indies. Little is known of his ancestry, but it is believed that he was a descendant of pioneer settlers who arrived on the island from England in the early eighteenth century. Thomas, a son of Samuel Mathews, immigrated to America in 1764 and settled in Norfolk, Virginia. Shortly thereafter, he studied law and was admitted to the bar. In 1773, he married Mollie Miller, with whom he had three children. With the clouds of war approaching, Mathews was a strong supporter of the revolutionary cause. He initially served as a militia lieutenant and possibly saw action at the Battle of Great Bridge in December 1775. He was then commissioned a captain in the Fourth Virginia Regiment on March 25, 1776, and served as a recruiting officer until his resignation on November 15, 1777. During part of that time, Mathews was also in command of Fort Nelson, which was built to protect Portsmouth and Gosport Shipyard from enemy attack. In November 1777, he was appointed as a major in the Virginia State Artillery Regiment commanded by Colonel Thomas Marshall, and he commanded local forces when British Major General Edward Mathew landed at Norfolk in May 1779 during his Chesapeake raid. Mathews also gained promotion to lieutenant colonel on November 8 that year. He continued to serve through 1781 and was actively engaged during the Siege of Yorktown. He went on to become an original member of the Society of the Cincinnati. Throughout the war, it was said that Mathews bore a striking resemblance to General Washington.

VIRGINIA MILITIA COMMANDERS AT YORKTOWN

Right: A depiction of Lieutenant Colonel Thomas Mathews painted in 1950 by one of his descendants, Ann S.V. Mann. *Mathews Memorial Library.*

Below: Following the Royal Navy attack on the USS *Chesapeake* in June 1807, Lieutenant Colonel Thomas Mathews helped develop harbor defenses for Norfolk. *Library of Congress.*

Even before the war's conclusion, Mathews had begun a new chapter of his public service career, forging into the world of politics. In May 1781, Norfolk residents elected him to serve in the Virginia House of Delegates, and he remained in office until May 1783. Mathews went on to again serve Norfolk in the House of Delegates from 1784 to 1794; 1797 to 1798; and 1799 to 1800. Moreover, he was chosen to serve as speaker of the house, a role he occupied from 1788—when he was also a member of the Virginia Ratifying Convention—to 1793. Interestingly, Mathews was the first speaker to serve in the current Virginia State Capitol Building in Richmond. Although he was considered a viable candidate for governor, he never served in that office. An active Mason, he was elected Grand Master of the Grand Lodge of Virginia in 1790 and served until 1793, when he was succeeded by John Marshall. That year, Mathews was also appointed a brigadier general in the Virginia militia; his headquarters were in Norfolk. In subsequent years, he continued to exert great influence as a prominent civic leader in his community. Mathews was also highly respected as an attorney and considered to be one of the leading members of the Norfolk Bar. His final chapter of public service occurred in June 1807, following the attack on the USS *Chesapeake* by the Royal Navy's HMS *Leopard*. What became known as the Chesapeake-Leopard Affair was a precipitating factor that eventually led to the War of 1812. In Norfolk, Mathews was integral in preparing harbor defenses while also serving as the head of the local committee of public safety. He passed away on February 20, 1812, following a long illness and was buried at St. Paul's Church in Norfolk. Mathews County, Virginia, founded in 1791, was named in his honor.

Chapter 14

LIEUTENANT COLONEL JOHN FRANCIS MERCER (1759–1821)

John Francis Mercer was a Virginia militia leader who had distinguished careers in both the military and political realms. He was also unique in that he accomplished these feats while serving two different states: Virginia and Maryland. Mercer was born on May 17, 1759, in Stafford County at his family's Marlborough Plantation. His father's parents, English-born John and Grace Mercer, had immigrated to Virginia from Ireland in 1720. His father, John Mercer, was a Dublin-born lawyer and planter who accumulated great wealth in Virginia before dying in debt. One of his brothers, Captain John Fenton Mercer, died during the French and Indian War while serving under George Washington, and a sister, Anna Mercer Harrison, was a sister-in-law of future President William Henry Harrison. Following his childhood in Stafford County, Mercer attended The College of William & Mary, where he read law with Thomas Jefferson and became close friends with fellow classmate James Monroe. After graduating in 1775, he was eager to support the patriot cause, and he joined the Third Virginia Regiment as an officer cadet a few months later. By February 1776, Mercer was a first lieutenant serving under Captain William Washington, and he may have fought at the Battle of Harlem Heights on September 16, 1776. The following year, he was wounded at the Battle of Brandywine and received a retroactive promotion to captain as of June 1777. Then, in June 1778, he left the Third Virginia Regiment to serve as aide-de-camp to Major General Charles Lee at the rank of major. Interestingly, Mercer was known for his steadfast loyalty to General

Lee and was by his side during Lee's professional demise at the Battle of Monmouth and subsequent court-martial. Adamantly opposed to how his boss was treated, Mercer resigned in protest from the Continental Army on July 2, 1779. General Lee never forgot that loyalty and would go on to remember Mercer in his will.

Meanwhile, Mercer went home to Marlborough for a time and then returned briefly to study law under Thomas Jefferson in Williamsburg. However, the war was shifting south, and he did not stay away from the battlefield for long. In October 1779, Mercer recruited a cavalry company for service in the Virginia militia and became a lieutenant colonel. In that capacity, he saw action at the Battle of Guilford Courthouse on March 15, 1781, serving in Brigadier General Robert Lawson's brigade. A short time later, Mercer attached himself to the Marquis de Lafayette's command and shifted his operations north to Virginia, where he fought at the Battle of Green Spring on July 6, 1781. At that engagement, Mercer led a small force of volunteer cavalry in heavy fighting against the British. During the Yorktown campaign, he played a pivotal role leading a force of grenadier militia under the overall command of Brigadier General George Weedon in Gloucester. Mercer's force, composed exclusively of Continental Army veterans, was the only one in Weedon's command that had any combat experience. It was therefore attached to the Duc de Lauzun's Legion and other French forces for active operations against the British in the area. In that capacity, Mercer and his grenadier militia played a major role in repelling British forces during the Battle of the Hook on October 3, 1781, which effectively bottled up the British at Gloucester Point for the remainder of the siege. A few days later, Mercer and his forces captured the advanced British redoubt, thereby tightening the noose. Then, on October 19, he was among those who took formal possession of the British works at Gloucester Point following their surrender.

With the war winding down, Mercer was elected to the Virginia House of Delegates, which in turn elected him as a delegate to the Continental

Lieutenant Colonel John Francis Mercer served as an aide-de-camp to Major General Charles Lee (shown here). Author's collection.

A painting depicting the Battle of the Hook by David Wagner. *Gloucester Museum of History.*

Congress. He served there until 1785, when he returned briefly to the House of Delegates. A year later, he married Sophia Sprigg and moved to Anne Arundel County, Maryland, where he became a Freemason and resided at the Cedar Park estate, which was Sophia's ancestral home. The couple went on to have four children together. Within two years of his arrival in the state, Mercer was active in Maryland politics, serving as a Maryland delegate to the Federal Constitutional Convention in 1787, where he opposed ratification. During this period, he published many of his views on the Constitution under the pseudonym "A Maryland Farmer." Gaining prominence in Anti-Federalist political circles, Mercer represented Anne Arundel County in the Maryland House of Delegates from 1788 to 1789 and again from 1791 to 1792. Shortly thereafter, he was elected to fill an unexpired term in the U.S. House of Representatives, and he served from 1792 to 1794. For the remainder of that decade, Mercer did not hold public office and tended instead to his interests at Cedar Park. However, he was elected again to the Maryland House of Delegates in 1800 and served there until his election as governor in 1801. Assuming office as part of an Anti-Federalist wave, Mercer was the first of several Virginians to be elected as Maryland's governor. Accomplishments during his tenure included the abolition of the property qualification for voting as well as the adoption of the secret ballot.

Lieutenant Colonel John Francis Mercer served as governor of Maryland from 1801 to 1803. *New York Public Library.*

After leaving office in 1803, Mercer returned to the Maryland House of Delegates and served there until 1806. Following that time, he concluded his political career and returned to Cedar Park. Prior to the War of 1812, Mercer reentered the public arena once more to align with the Federalists in an effort to avoid conflict with England. A few years later, in failing health, he traveled to Philadelphia to consult with doctors, and he died there in August 1821. His funeral was attended by a number of prominent Philadelphia citizens. Buried initially in a vault at St. Peter's Church in that city, he was later moved to Cedar Park. Mercer left behind a large financial estate, including seventy-three enslaved persons. Though Mercer was a slave owner, some of his relatives went on to actively oppose the institution. For instance, his daughter Margaret Mercer was a noted abolitionist and educator who operated a school in Loudoun County, Virginia, that welcomed Black students. Mercer's nephew Charles F. Mercer was a longtime U.S. congressman who also opposed slavery. He helped establish the American Colonization Society in 1816. In another time and arena, one of Mercer's descendants was also historically notable. Lucy Mercer Rutherford, a direct descendant through Mercer's son John, was known in the twentieth century for her close relationship with President Franklin D. Roosevelt.

Chapter 15

COLONEL THOMAS MERIWETHER (UNCERTAIN)

It is clear in the historical record that there was a Colonel Thomas Meriwether who commanded Virginia militia forces during the Siege of Yorktown. He led a regiment that was part of Brigadier General Edward Stevens's brigade. However, as in the case of Colonel William Lewis, it is difficult to identify the specific Thomas Meriwether who performed that service, considering that the Meriwethers were a prolific Virginia family at that time and there was several Thomas Meriwethers in the area. The most likely candidate is Thomas Meriwether of Louisa County, who was born on September 9, 1752. He was a son of Captain David H. Meriwether (and his wife, Mary), a sea captain who was lost in the Atlantic Ocean in 1772, only seven days out from Yorktown en route to Bristol, England. Interestingly, Thomas Meriwether was a second cousin of Meriwether Lewis of Lewis and Clark Expedition fame. Moreover, Meriwether County, Georgia, was named for another distant cousin, Virginia-born Brigadier General David Meriwether, who served in the Continental Army as well as in the Georgia militia following the war. General Meriwether also served Georgia as a member of the U.S. House of Representatives from 1802 to 1807.

Meriwether Lewis (*shown here*), of Lewis and Clark Expedition fame, was likely a second cousin of Colonel Thomas Meriwether. *Library of Congress.*

On November 25, 1776, Thomas Meriwether was appointed a captain in the Virginia State Marine Corps. Shortly thereafter, he was appointed a captain in the First Virginia Regiment on February 1, 1777, gaining promotion to major on June 1, 1778. Meriwether likely saw action at the Battles of Brandywine, Germantown and Monmouth. He served on the Continental Line until February 1781 and may have secured appointment as a militia colonel in the weeks thereafter, setting the stage for service at Yorktown. Meriwether was reportedly an expert marksman, and in that capacity, he may have been selected to serve during the siege. For his efforts, Meriwether was later awarded 5,333 acres of land, presumably in Georgia. His brother, Lieutenant James Meriwether, was similarly awarded land for his wartime services as adjutant in the First Virginia Regiment. Following the war, Thomas Meriwether moved to Jefferson County, Georgia, where he passed away on March 18, 1803. His place of burial is unknown. It does not appear that Meriwether married or had children, for in his will, only his brother James and several nieces are named as beneficiaries. As in the case of the aforementioned Colonel William Lewis, further research is needed to learn more about Meriwether's service at Yorktown as well as during other points of the war.

Chapter 16

BRIGADIER GENERAL THOMAS NELSON JR. (1738–1789)

Thomas Nelson is undoubtedly the most prominent and well-remembered militia officer to have served during the Siege of Yorktown. During that operation, he performed dual roles, as the Commonwealth's senior militia commander as well as its governor. Nelson also had the ironic distinction of helping lay siege to his own hometown. Overall, he was a Founding Father who played a pivotal role in supporting his native state throughout the American Revolution. The eldest of five sons, Nelson was born on December 26, 1738, to an aristocratic Tidewater Virginia family that had long been situated in Yorktown. His grandfather Thomas "Scotch Tom" Nelson had emigrated from Cumberland, England, in the early eighteenth century and played an integral role in developing Yorktown. Meanwhile, Nelson's father, William Nelson, served as a colonial legislator, judge and royal governor but actively supported the patriot cause in the years leading up to the Revolutionary War. Nelson's mother, Elizabeth Carter Burwell, also descended from a prominent Virginia family, being a daughter of Robert "King" Carter.

Descending from such notable bloodlines, Nelson grew up amid wealth and privilege and also received an excellent preparatory education. During his teenage years, he was tutored by the Reverend William Yates of Gloucester, who later served as president of The College of William & Mary. As a member of the planter elite, Nelson had the opportunity to study in England, where he graduated from Christ's College, Cambridge, in 1760. On returning home to Virginia in 1761, he developed a close relationship with Lucy Grymes of Williamsburg, whom he married the following August. With robust financial support from Nelson's parents, the young couple established themselves in Yorktown and went on to have eleven children together. Interestingly, five of those children would go on to marry children of Gloucester County's Colonel John Page. Meanwhile, Nelson began to immerse himself in civic affairs, serving as a justice of the peace and as a member the House of Burgesses through the early 1770s. After the passing of his father in 1772, he was also active with his brother Hugh in overseeing the family's business ventures. However, the onset of war in the mid-1770s prompted Nelson to devote his full attention to the political arena. In 1774, he was appointed as one of Virginia's delegates to the First Continental Congress. The following year, he served as a member of the second Virginia Provincial Convention, where he successfully advocated for the creation of two Virginia militia regiments. He and Patrick Henry were then named as commanders of those units. A short time later, Nelson served as a delegate to the Second Continental Congress, where he was a strong advocate for independence from Great Britain. He therefore voted in favor of the Declaration of Independence on July 2, 1776, which forever enshrined him as one of the nation's Founding Fathers.

As the war progressed, Nelson committed large sums from his personal coffers to support the patriot cause. Moreover, he shared his own horses to transport supplies and ammunition and his own land to grow food for the troops. Although he was an active member of the Continental Congress, the lingering effects of a mild stroke forced him to retire in May 1777. Following a period of recuperation, he regained enough health to accept appointment as a brigadier general commanding all Virginia militia forces in August 1777. However, as the threat of possible British invasion passed, his command was deactivated by the end of the following month. Nelson later assumed command of the Lower Virginia militia in 1778. During that

RES. OF THOMAS NELSON JR. YORKTOWN VA

Opposite: Brigadier General Thomas Nelson Jr. from an original 1754 portrait. *New York Public Library.*

Above: The residence of Brigadier General Thomas Nelson Jr. in Yorktown. *New York Public Library.*

time, he also formed a cavalry unit at his own expense and rode toward Philadelphia with the intention of joining General Washington's main army. However, by the time they arrived in camp, their service was ultimately deemed unnecessary, and they were ordered to return home with the thanks of Congress. Prior to leaving for Virginia, Nelson presented a fine horse as a gift to General Washington, a kind gesture that was sincerely appreciated by the commander in chief. Nelson then returned to the Continental Congress in 1779, but a relapse of illness forced him to retire once again after only a few months. In the meantime, Nelson tended to personal business matters by purchasing a 5,400-acre plantation in Prince William County that also included enslaved persons.

As before, Nelson was able to resume political and military service back in Virginia following a period of recovery. By that time, war had arrived on his doorstep, and he was consequently active in trying to repel the various British incursions in 1780 and 1781. This frequently involved making inspection tours of the Tidewater area, where Nelson advocated regularly for stronger defenses. He also worked closely with Governor Thomas Jefferson and the

Baron von Steuben, who commanded all Virginia-based forces at the time. In February 1781, Nelson was even briefly involved in a plan to capture Benedict Arnold, but the operation was called off as strategic priorities began to change. When Jefferson declined to seek reelection as governor, Nelson was selected to succeed him in June 1781. As before, Nelson committed large sums of his own money and materials to support Virginia's troops.

Faced with the growing British threat, Nelson ordered officials in several northwestern Virginia counties to mobilize militia to join the growing forces under the Marquis de Lafayette, who succeeded von Steuben as the overall military commander in the region. In his dual roles as governor and brigadier general, Nelson struggled to maintain order amid the public panic over British attacks in the area. By July 1781, he had ordered Colonel James Innes to establish a defensive post in Williamsburg with an eye toward providing some degree of protection for the Virginia Peninsula area. Meanwhile, Nelson also struggled to find ways to supply the growing patriot forces as they began to maneuver toward Yorktown. On September 14, 1781, he helped escort General Washington into Williamsburg, who then set up his headquarters at the Wythe House. Nelson also busily attended to the logistical preparations necessary to facilitate the forthcoming Siege of Yorktown.

On September 28, 1781, the Allied Army, composed of over sixteen thousand troops total, began to make its way to Yorktown from its camps in Williamsburg. Nelson commanded the three-thousand-strong Virginia militia forces, which were organized into three brigades commanded by Brigadier Generals George Weedon, Robert Lawson and Edward Stevens. In the following days, Nelson strove to provide supply and logistical support for the large Allied Army—a difficult task. His forces also had to hastily cut down trees and dig entrenchments to keep up with the rapidly evolving strategic situation. Meanwhile, Nelson had to contend with his uncle Thomas Nelson Sr. (known as the Secretary) being trapped in his besieged Yorktown home. Fortunately, an appeal by Nelson and his relatives to General Washington resulted in a flag of truce being arranged for October 10, 1781, which allowed for Secretary Nelson to leave the home and cross over to the American lines. The same day, as Allied artillery pounded the British positions in Yorktown, Nelson encouraged the artillerists to fire on his own home, which Lord Cornwallis was using as his headquarters. He reportedly even offered five guineas apiece to gunners who managed to actually hit the residence.

On October 17, the British finally sought a cessation of hostilities, and the siege began to come to a close. Two days later, Nelson joined the senior Continental Army and French commanders in accepting the British surrender. Although he paused briefly to accept praise from General Washington for a job well done, Nelson quickly went back to work sending communiques and making arrangements for transport of the British prisoners. He also had to make logistical arrangements for the French troops who would be stationed in the region for several more months. The frantic pace no doubt contributed to a relapse of his illness, and Nelson began to suffer from labored breathing and chronic chest congestion. He therefore resigned the governorship, citing ill health, on November 21, 1781. While convalescing in Hanover County in early 1782, Nelson entertained several distinguished guests, including General Rochambeau. Warmer weather gradually brought a degree of renewed health, and Nelson was once again reelected to the Virginia House of Delegates. However, his colleagues in the legislature quickly noticed that the frequent bouts of illness had taken a toll on Nelson's stamina.

Following the war, Nelson began to step back from public life. However, as the 1780s progressed, he did serve several more terms in the House of Delegates. With most of his fortune gone, he was unable to commit the funds necessary to resume his previous life in Yorktown, which had been ravaged by war. Nelson therefore moved with his family to Williamsburg in 1783, though he quickly came to realize that it was not the same town it was in the prewar era. In subsequent years, Nelson occupied himself with legislative service while also trying in vain to improve his financial situation. To pay off debts, he sold off vast holdings, including land as well as enslaved persons. Meanwhile, as his health steadily declined, asthmatic chest congestion and coughing made it increasingly difficult for him to breathe. Nelson later retired to his Hanover County estate, known as Offley Hoo, where he passed away from illness on January 4, 1789—only a few days after

A depiction of Brigadier General Thomas Nelson Jr. in his later years. *New York Public Library.*

reaching the age of fifty. He had not been present during the Constitutional Convention but was reportedly opposed to ratification, presumably believing that it was too invasive of states' rights. Nelson's widow, Lucy, survived him by many years but spent the remainder of her life in poverty and poor health. They are both interred at Grace Episcopal Church in Yorktown. Their Yorktown home remained in the Nelson family until 1914, when it was acquired by new owners, who later renovated the home and renamed it York Hall. It was subsequently acquired by the National Park Service in 1968. Today, it is known as the Nelson House, and as part of the Colonial National Park, it is open to the public. Nelson County, Virginia, and Nelson County, Kentucky, are both named in his honor. Virginia's Thomas Nelson Community College, established in 1967, was also named for Nelson (it was renamed Virginia Peninsula Community College in 2022). Interestingly, Nelson was a third cousin of George Washington, though it is unclear whether the pair ever knew that they were related.

Chapter 17

COLONEL WILLIAM NELSON

(1746–1807)

William Nelson was born on June 17, 1746, in Yorktown, the eldest son of Thomas Nelson Sr. and his wife, Lucy Armistead. Thomas Nelson Sr., often referred to as the Secretary, had served as the secretary of the Virginia Colony from 1743 to 1776. The Nelsons therefore wielded enormous influence in Yorktown and its surrounding areas. Following a refined childhood, William Nelson went on to study in England alongside his first cousin, the future Virginia Governor Thomas Nelson Jr. He married Lucy Chiswell of Caroline County on November 24, 1770, and thereafter settled in Hanover County. Residing at their estate, known as the Dorrill, they would go on to have seven children together. Professionally, he occupied himself during this time by serving as Caroline County clerk, a profitable position that had been arranged for by his father. However, as war was fast approaching, Nelson put aside his domestic life to serve in the Continental Army. He was appointed a major in the Seventh Virginia Regiment in January 1776 and promoted to lieutenant colonel in October that year. During this period, Nelson saw action in the New York Campaign as well as at the Battle of Brandywine the following year. Regrettably, Nelson's wartime service is often confused with that of his cousin Judge William Nelson (1754–1813), who held the ranks of captain, major and lieutenant colonel in the Seventh Virginia Regiment. However, sources are clear in stating that the subject of this piece resigned from the Continental Army in the fall of 1777. In an October 13 letter to General Washington, Nelson explained that pressing private and family responsibilities required

Colonel William Nelson fought at the Battle of Brandywine on September 11, 1777. *Library of Congress.*

him to return to Virginia. Back home, he believed, he could still serve his country while tending to his own affairs.

In that spirit, Nelson remained an active supporter of the patriot cause. In December 1779, he joined fellow Continental Army veterans Samuel Griffin and James Innes in helping recruit new troops. Then, in 1780, Nelson's cousin Governor Thomas Nelson assigned him command of a state regiment that would operate in the vicinity of Yorktown. By June 1781, his forces were encamped at Leedstown, which is a small community in modern-day Westmoreland County. In the following weeks, Nelson proceeded to Yorktown to take part in the siege. It is unclear whether he commanded troops at Yorktown or whether he perhaps served his cousin Governor Thomas Nelson in a staff or advisory capacity. Regardless, Nelson was actively engaged in what must have been quite a surreal assault on his hometown. Worried about his father, who was trapped in Yorktown, Nelson lobbied General Washington for a temporary truce to get the secretary evacuated. This took place on October 10, much to the relief of Nelson and the rest of his family. Following the siege and the subsequent British surrender, Nelson returned home to the Dorrill to tend to his growing family—roughly nine of his children were born after the war. He passed away on November 24, 1807, and was buried in King William County.

Chapter 18

COLONEL JOHN PAGE

(1743-1808)

John Page was a distinguished Virginian who made important societal contributions across multiple fields of endeavor. Page is also sometimes remembered for his connection to the historic Rosewell plantation in Gloucester County, which was built by his grandfather Mann Page I. John, born at Rosewell on April 28, 1743, was a son of Mann and Alice (Grymes) Page II and a great-great-grandson of Colonel John Page (1628–1692), a wealthy English-born merchant who helped establish Williamsburg as Virginia's capital in 1698. Following his mother's passing when he was only three, Page was raised by his paternal grandmother, Judith Carter Page, who instilled in him a lifelong love of learning. Although he was originally slated to study in England, Page was enrolled instead at The College of William & Mary, where he studied classics and lived for several years with the College's president. As the scion of a prominent Virginia family, Page met several notable figures during his time at William & Mary, including Governors Dinwiddie, Fauquier, Botetourt and Dunmore. However, the most significant and lasting connection was the one he made with fellow classmate Thomas Jefferson, with whom Page established a close friendship. This bond would prove crucial to Page's professional advancement in later years.

Following Page's graduation from William & Mary in 1763, he accompanied George Washington as a junior officer on a western expedition against the French and their Indian allies. Two years later, he married Frances Burwell and was given Rosewell in the process as a gift from his father. The couple would go on to have twelve children, of whom seven would survive to maturity. Interestingly, five of them would later marry children of Governor Thomas Nelson, helping forge a strong multigenerational bond between those families. In 1765, Page was also appointed a justice of the peace for Gloucester County, and he served a short time later as a member of William & Mary's Board of Visitors. Then, in 1771, he was elected to the House of Burgesses, and shortly thereafter, he was appointed to the Governor's Council. Although Page's political prospects looked bright during this period, he encountered some challenges closer to home. Extensive renovations to Rosewell combined with depleting crop productivity conspired to put him in dire financial straits. The situation grew worse as war with the British approached, depriving Page of the lucrative British tobacco market for his crops. Finding solace in the world of science, Page helped organize a local chapter of the Philosophical Society in Williamsburg in 1773. He went on to serve as the chapter's vice president and president as it grew to over one hundred members. In this capacity, Page was active in researching astronomy and even invented a device that could measure the amount of rain that fell over time. He was also an active member of the Anglican Church and was widely respected by his peers for his knowledge of theological doctrine. Some held him in such high regard in this realm that they even recommended that Page serve as Virginia's first bishop.

Thomas Jefferson was a close friend and supporter of Colonel John Page. *New York Public Library.*

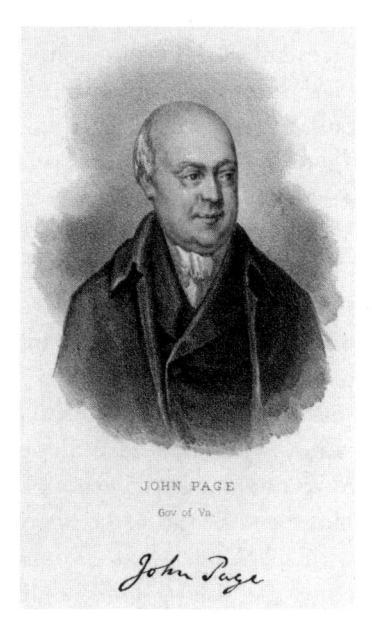

Colonel John Page. *New York Public Library.*

However, the coming war with Great Britain prompted Page to shift his focus to political and military matters. As a member of the Committee of Public Safety in 1775, he was an early advocate for the development of a Virginia navy. He was also nominated to serve as Virginia's first elected governor, later losing that potential distinction to Patrick Henry. Nevertheless, Page was chosen in 1776 to serve on the Governor's Council and was also elected by the council to serve as lieutenant governor. In that capacity, he received official notification from John Hancock on July 20, 1776, about the signing of the Declaration of Independence. During this period, Page returned to Rosewell whenever he could and advocated for increased defenses for Gloucester. Thomas Jefferson was a frequent visitor to Rosewell, and popular legend holds that he wrote an early draft of the Declaration of Independence while staying at the Page estate. The pair even ran against each other in an amicable campaign for governor in 1779, which Jefferson won by a small margin. While Page forged ahead in his public service roles, that service continued to come at the expense of his business interests and financial affairs at Rosewell. The situation was exacerbated in 1780 when he took in four of his sister's children following their father's passing. Caring for these children as well as his own created an acute financial strain that compelled him to resign from the Governor's Council that April. Furthermore, Page refused to be considered as a candidate to succeed Jefferson as governor.

Ironically, Page's retirement from public life proved to be short-lived, as the war came to his doorstep. Appointed a colonel in the Gloucester County militia, he was active in the defense of the Virginia Peninsula during Benedict Arnold's foray up the James River in 1781. He continued serving in this capacity during the Siege of Yorktown, when he commanded a regiment in Brigadier General George Weedon's brigade. On September 17, 1781, Page was ordered to move his force of four hundred troops to Poplar Spring Church to support area forces and reconnoiter the British positions closer to Gloucester Point. Page and his regiment thus played a key role in assisting American and French forces and in protecting area inhabitants from British foraging parties.

Following the British surrender at Yorktown, Page immediately returned to his political pursuits. He was elected to the House of Delegates in late 1781 and later served on the Pennsylvania-Virginia Boundary Commission in 1784. In that role, he utilized his skills in making astrological calculations to help extend the Mason-Dixon Line. Sadly, his wife, Frances, passed away in 1784, along with his son John. He remarried a short time later and, with encouragement from Thomas Jefferson, continued his bids for public office. From 1785 to 1788, Page served in the Virginia House of Delegates,

ROSEWELL.

Rosewell was located in Gloucester County. Thomas Jefferson may have written an early draft of the Declaration of Independence there. *New York Public Library.*

and from 1789 to 1797, he served in the U.S. House of Representatives. Defeated for reelection, Page returned to the House of Delegates briefly before losing reelection there as well. However, after Jefferson's ascendancy to the presidency, Page's political prospects improved considerably. Succeeding James Monroe, he was elected governor of Virginia in 1802 and won reelection two times. Following his gubernatorial administration, Page served as United States commissioner of loans for Virginia. He passed away on October 11, 1808, and was buried at St. John's Episcopal Church in Richmond. Page County, Virginia, established in 1831, was named in his honor.

Chapter 19

COLONEL SIR JOHN PEYTON

(1720–1790)

Sir John Peyton was unique among his Tidewater Virginia contemporaries in that even as a titled member of the English nobility, he zealously supported the revolutionary cause. Born in 1720 in Gloucester County, he was the son of Thomas and Francis (Tabb) Peyton of Isleham, a plantation located in modern-day Mathews County. Peyton's grandfather Major Robert Peyton established Isleham in the 1680s, naming it after the Peyton estate in Cambridgeshire, England, where he grew up. It is unclear when Peyton assumed his family's baronetcy, which was created on May 22, 1611, by King James I. He became heir to it on the death of a relative, Sir John Peyton, the Fourth Baronet, who died without issue in England in 1721. However, records indicate that Peyton was using the title as early as 1756. By 1758, he was also a captain in the Gloucester County militia. During this period, Peyton had nine children by his first wife, Frances (who passed away in 1778), and one child, who died in infancy, with his second wife, Mary. He was an active leader in the Episcopal Church, serving as a vestryman and warden at his local parish. In the business realm, Peyton prospered by raising tobacco and cattle. When hostilities with Great Britain commenced, Peyton was quick to join the revolutionary cause. He was an original member of the Gloucester Committee of Safety that was formed in the war's early stages. Peyton was then appointed colonel of the Gloucester County militia on September 13, 1775, and he contributed extensively to the war effort. For instance, he was celebrated for personally guaranteeing payment of $60,000 in inflated Continental currency for 250 stands of arms to help equip Gloucester

County troops in 1781. This action earned him the distinction of being called the Gloucester County Patriot. However, he came into trouble when the supplier, Adam Van Bibber & Company of Baltimore, demanded payment, which Peyton lacked the funds to provide. The Commonwealth of Virginia later reimbursed Peyton for this expenditure, though not until after a lawsuit was brought against him by the supplier and judgement secured, causing Peyton great embarrassment.

Leading up to and during the Siege of Yorktown, Peyton spent much of his time procuring supplies for the American forces, serving within Brigadier General George Weedon's area of operations in Gloucester. In particular, Governor Thomas Nelson requested his assistance in securing boats in August 1781 and beef and salt the following month. Peyton was also active in lobbying state authorities for assistance, owing to Gloucester's exposed status to enemy foraging raids and other threats. He continued his public service following the war, serving as Gloucester County sheriff from 1782 to 1783, a role that at the time was akin to county administrator. One of his responsibilities as sheriff was to collect taxes. However, in those lean economic years, most people were unable to pay, and as per the laws of the time, Peyton became personally indebted for the delinquent taxes. Facing abject poverty, he appealed to state authorities for assistance in a legal dispute that took years to sort out. Despite these challenges, Peyton still possessed significant holdings in what is now Mathews County, including 2 employees, 128 enslaved persons, 28 horses and 120 cattle. He died suddenly on March 25, 1790, leaving behind his wife, Lady Mary, as administrator to sort out his estate. Peyton was buried at his beloved Isleham, which was eventually sold out of the Peyton family in 1813.

King James I created Colonel Sir John Peyton's family baronetcy in 1611. *Library of Congress.*

Chapter 20

COLONEL BEVERLEY RANDOLPH

(1754-1797)

Beverley Randolph was born in 1754 in Henrico County on his family's estate, Chatsworth. He was a son of House of Burgesses member Peter Randolph and his wife, Lucy Bolling Randolph, who both descended from historically prominent Virginia families. Randolph attended The College of William & Mary in the early 1770s and married Martha Cocke of Williamsburg in 1775, later having one daughter with her. Though faced with debilitating hereditary gout, Randolph was in active military service for much of the Revolutionary War. As a William & Mary student, he marched in 1775 as a volunteer to help prevent the seizure of public stores by Lord Dunmore's forces in Williamsburg. Settling a short time later in Cumberland County, he served on the Cumberland County Committee of Public Safety and commanded a local cavalry regiment as a colonel between 1776 and 1779. In addition, Randolph served in the Virginia House of Delegates in 1777 as well as from 1779 to 1781, when he was appointed to the Virginia Council of State. In March that year, he commanded a Virginia militia regiment in Brigadier General Robert Lawson's brigade at the Battle of Guilford Courthouse, leading troops from Powhatan, Amelia and Cumberland Counties. Randolph and his men withstood, for a time, heavy attack from advancing British forces, and Randolph received Major General Nathanael Greene's public gratitude following the battle. During the Siege of Yorktown, Randolph continued to lead the Cumberland County militia and was assigned again to Brigadier General Robert Lawson's brigade. Sadly, since a postwar fire at Chatsworth destroyed

Randolph's letters and papers, additional details concerning his wartime service are no longer known.

Following the war, Randolph continued his government service, winning election as president of the Council of State in 1783 and again from 1786 to 1788. In that capacity, he essentially served as Virginia's lieutenant governor. He also served as a member of William & Mary's Board of Visitors in 1784. He then succeeded his relative Edmund Randolph as governor of Virginia in 1788, winning election to additional one-year terms in 1789 and 1790. He was, therefore, the first governor elected following Virginia's ratification of the Constitution. During Randolph's gubernatorial administration, he focused on defending the frontier against Indian incursions and lobbied to collect Virginia's outstanding Revolutionary War claims from the federal government. He also led an initiative to build a lighthouse at the entrance of the Chesapeake Bay. Additional milestones during his administration were the Virginia General Assembly's decisions to cede land to help establish the District of Columbia and to begin the process of Kentucky becoming an independent state. Following his terms as governor, Randolph was appointed in 1793 by President Washington to serve as a commissioner to help secure a treaty with Indians in the Northwest Territory. However, when that effort failed, Randolph retired from public life. He passed away on February 7, 1797, at his estate called Green Creek in Cumberland County and was buried there. However, in 1909, his remains were reinterred at Westview Cemetery in Farmville, Virginia.

Major General Nathanael Greene (*pictured*) extended his public gratitude to Colonel Beverley Randolph for his valiant service during the Battle of Guilford Courthouse. *New York Public Library.*

Chapter 21

COLONEL HOLT RICHESON
(1736–1800)

Holt Richeson was born on September 30, 1736, to a family that had long been situated in New Kent County. His father, James Richeson, moved to King William County at some point in the early eighteenth century and established a home near Bull Swamp called Kentuckie, which went on to become an 875-acre plantation. Richeson's surname was likely a shortened form of Richardson, as church records connect that name to some of his close relatives. As a young adult, Richeson settled in King William County, where he married his first wife, Susanna. She was a daughter of Colonel Francis West, a French and Indian War veteran and descendant of Thomas West, Second Baron De La Warr, who had served as a House of Burgesses member and King William County sheriff. The couple later resided at Kentuckie, and they had eight children together prior to Susanna's death in 1780. Richeson would later marry a second wife, Elizabeth Hogg of King and Queen County, with whom he would have five additional children.

Richeson was an early and active participant in the Revolutionary War. In 1775, he was dispatched by then Colonel Patrick Henry to Laneville, the home of prominent loyalist Colonel Richard Corbin, with orders to arrest him. When Richeson and his troops arrived at Laneville to find that Corbin had escaped, they rushed through West Point to join the militia forces organizing at Doncastle's Ordinary in James City County. Thereafter, he served with distinction for several years in the Continental Army. He was commissioned a captain in the Seventh Virginia Regiment on February 26, 1776, and quickly promoted to major in the Fifteenth Virginia Regiment in

November that year. During this time, he led several operations throughout Virginia in pursuit of the British army. On October 7, 1777, Richeson was promoted to lieutenant colonel and transferred back to the Seventh Virginia Regiment, where he would later see action at the Battle of Monmouth. Then, in July 1778, he was sent to Williamsburg with other field grade officers to oversee the recruiting of new troops. In November that year, Richeson was transferred to the Fifth Virginia Regiment, where he continued his field service. However, like so many other officers, Richeson felt the strain of trying to support a young wife and family from afar. In an April 1779 letter to General Washington, he lamented that his meager pay could no longer adequately provide for his dependents. He therefore resigned his commission in May 1779 and returned to King William County.

However, Richeson's public service continued: King William voters elected him around that time to serve in the Virginia House of Delegates. Colleagues such as Edmund Pendleton expressed reservations about this role transition, wondering whether Richeson would be as good a legislator as he was a soldier. However, the British operations in Virginia brought him back into military service in 1781, and at the Siege of Yorktown, Richeson commanded a militia regiment in Brigadier General Robert Lawson's brigade. Moreover, according to Richeson's aide-de-camp, Captain Humphrey Brooke, Richeson

Colonel Holt Richeson saw action at the Battle of Monmouth, which was fought on June 28, 1778. *New York Public Library.*

even commanded the brigade during parts of the siege in Lawson's absence. Following the war, Richeson returned to King William County, where he continued his tenure as a state legislator until 1782. In 1788, he was a member of the Virginia Constitutional Convention, and he served during that period as King William County's deputy sheriff. Around this time, Richeson also sold Kentuckie; he later resided at Tuckoman as well as at another plantation near Cohoke Mill. Following Richeson's death in 1800, some of his children and grandchildren migrated out to Kentucky, settling in Mason County. One of his sons, John Brett Richeson, went on to become a prominent Kentucky educator and established Maysville Academy, which counted among its students a young Ulysses S. Grant. Richeson's place of burial is unknown.

Chapter 22

LIEUTENANT COLONEL HENRY SKIPWITH

(1751–1815)

Henry Skipwith was one of several Virginia militia commanders who had distinguished familial roots in the English gentry. The Virginia branch of this family descended from the Skipwiths of Prestwould, located in Leicestershire, England. His ancestor Sir Henry Skipwith was created a baronet by King James I in 1622 and was later a royalist and acquaintance of King Charles I during the English Civil War. Sir Henry's son Sir Grey Skipwith, Third Baronet of Prestwould, immigrated to Virginia around 1657 and settled in what is now Middlesex County. Henry Skipwith was a younger brother to the Seventh Baronet of Prestwould and was born in Prince George County in 1751. His parents, Sir William and Sarah (Peyton) Skipwith, resided at Prestwould Plantation in Mecklenburg County. Following a childhood spent in southside Virginia, he married Anne Wayles on July 7, 1773, and went on to have at least three children with her. Anne was a sister of Thomas Jefferson's wife, Martha, making Skipwith Jefferson's brother-in-law. Skipwith and Jefferson grew close in subsequent years and exchanged voluminous correspondence. Joined by their brother-in-law Francis Eppes, the pair also served as executors of their father-in-law John Wayles's estate following his death in May 1773. During this period, Skipwith and his family resided at their plantation called Hors du Monde, which was located near the Appomattox River in Cumberland County.

Despite his aristocratic roots in the English gentry, Skipwith became an active supporter of the patriot cause. He was appointed an officer in the Cumberland County militia in 1776 and quickly rose to the rank of major.

Lieutenant Colonel Henry Skipwith spent his later years living in the Wythe House in Williamsburg, where he moved in 1798. *New York Public Library.*

Skipwith also served as the county magistrate for much of the same period. Following the American defeat at the Battle of Camden in August 1780, Skipwith was among the militia forces mobilized to help support Major General Nathanael Greene's campaign in the Carolinas. By March 1781, he was serving under Greene's command in Colonel Robert Munford's regiment of Brigadier General Robert Lawson's brigade. When a case of gout sidelined Munford, command of the regiment went to Skipwith, who subsequently saw action at the Battle of Guilford Courthouse. Skipwith's unit suffered heavy casualties at the hands of the British Grenadiers and Second Guards Battalion but fought admirably. Following Guilford Courthouse, he was ordered to join the Marquis de Lafayette's growing forces north of the James River in modern-day Hanover County. As a lieutenant colonel, Skipwith went on to command a militia regiment in Lawson's brigade during the Siege of Yorktown. Around October 15, Skipwith and his forces were subjected to a surprise British sortie while guarding American artillery along the siege line. Although the British attempted to spike the guns, Skipwith's forces held their own, and a counterattack led by the Count de Noailles and his French troops drove the British back.

 Following the war, Skipwith returned to Cumberland County, where, in 1782, voters elected him to serve in the Virginia House of Delegates. Following Anne's death in 1798, he married Elizabeth Byrd and moved to Williamsburg, where they lived in the George Wythe House, named after the previous owner, who was a famed jurist and signer of the Declaration of Independence. Among Skipwith's neighbors and close friends were fellow Siege of Yorktown veteran St. George Tucker. During this time, Skipwith was frequently visited by his brother Sir Peyton Skipwith and his wife, Lady Ann Skipwith, who went on to become the subject of popular ghost stories in Williamsburg. Her apparition can supposedly still be seen and heard throughout the Wythe House to this day. Skipwith lived a quiet life until his death in Powhatan County in 1815. His place of burial is unknown. Elizabeth continued residing in Williamsburg until her own passing in 1819. Interestingly, one of Skipwith's cousins, a fellow Revolutionary War veteran named Fulwar Skipwith, was a key player in negotiating the Louisiana Purchase in 1803. He also served as governor of the short-lived Republic of West Florida in 1810.

Chapter 23

Brigadier General Edward Stevens
(1745–1820)

Although he is not as widely remembered as some of his fellow Virginia-born officers, Culpeper County native Edward Stevens had a distinguished record during the American Revolution, seeing action in both the northern and southern theaters. Born in 1745, Stevens spent his entire childhood in the Culpeper area, which became a county in 1749. His parents were among the first settlers of British descent to establish themselves in that region. It is not clear whether Stevens grew up to be a farmer or a merchant, but he may have dabbled in both fields. At some point before 1769, he married Gizzell (Gilly) Coleman, with whom he eventually had three children. As war with Great Britain approached, it can be assumed based on his later actions that Stevens was an ardent supporter of the patriot cause.

In the fall of 1775, Stevens was appointed a lieutenant colonel, and he served as second in command (under Colonel Lawrence Taliaferro) of the Culpeper Minutemen. This unit consisted of approximately 350 men raised from Culpeper, Orange and Fauquier Counties. That October, they made their way to Williamsburg to join other minutemen who were organizing to oppose the forces of Virginia's royal governor, Lord Dunmore. Shortly thereafter, Colonel William Woodford, the commander of patriot troops in the area, sent Stevens and 100 men on a scouting mission to British-held Fort Murray, located in the Great Bridge section of modern-day Chesapeake. Following some initial skirmishing on December 4, Stevens and his force were instrumental in the Battle of Great Bridge, which was fought five days later. Stevens then continued his valorous service by leading bold attacks against British forces as they attempted to burn Norfolk's waterfront area on January 1, 1776. For the next several months, Stevens remained active in efforts to oppose Lord Dunmore's forces, who were driven out of Virginia in August 1776. These efforts were rewarded in January 1777, when he was appointed a Continental Army colonel in command of the newly organized Tenth Virginia Regiment, which was composed of troops from several northwestern Virginia counties. Serving in Brigadier General George Weedon's brigade, the Tenth Virginia spent the spring and summer months encamped at Morristown and Bound Brook, New Jersey. During that period, Stevens also engaged in administrative assignments, including service as presiding officer of a general court-martial that June.

On September 11, 1777, Stevens returned to the battlefield when his regiment served at the Battle of Brandywine. While the Tenth Virginia was involved only on the periphery during the main battle, Stevens and his men, along with Pennsylvania forces commanded by Colonel Walter Stewart, provided cover for the Continental Army's retreat and engaged in fierce fighting against the advancing British forces. Less than a month

Brigadier General Edward Stevens saw action at the Battle of Germantown, which was fought on October 4, 1777. *New York Public Library.*

later, Stevens once again saw action, at the Battle of Germantown, fought on October 4. Although a navigational error resulted in Weedon's brigade arriving late to the fighting, Stevens and his troops were heavily involved in pushing back advancing British forces until a general withdrawal was ordered. One wounded officer later claimed that Stevens personally carried him off the battlefield. Stevens later moved into the encampment at Valley Forge, expecting to pass an uneventful winter with his troops. However, the break in action was interrupted on January 20, 1778, when a force of two hundred British dragoons raided the area where Stevens was staying in Radnor, Pennsylvania, and attempted to capture him. To the surprise of the British force, Stevens and his troops fought back ferociously, prompting them to withdraw. Nevertheless, Stevens's forces continued to advance and even captured a significant number of the dragoons as well as their horses. This successful operation only added to the valorous reputation of Stevens and his men. Despite these accolades, frustration over a denied furlough prompted Stevens to resign from the Continental Army in January 1778. It would be two more years before he would return to active military service.

In response to the disastrous events in South Carolina that culminated in the American surrender at Charleston, the Virginia General Assembly called up a force of 2,500 militiamen to be sent south. Stevens was appointed a brigadier general and took command of this force. In June 1780, Stevens advanced to Hillsborough, North Carolina, and spent the next several weeks training his raw and inexperienced troops, which by then numbered about 1,625 men. Then, on August 13, Stevens linked up with his new commanding officer, Major General Horatio Gates, at Rugeley's Mills. They encountered British troops under Lord Cornwallis sooner than expected, so Gates held a war council with his senior officers to ponder their next move on the eve of the impending battle. After Gates asked whether it was better to fight or withdraw, the fearless Stevens boldly asserted that they had to fight, as the opportunity had already passed for them to leave. Meanwhile, officers who favored withdrawing were reluctant to speak, and this hesitation therefore helped foreshadow the disastrous Battle of Camden. During that August 16 engagement, terrified Virginia militiamen broke ranks and fled despite Stevens's best efforts to rally them. An infuriated Stevens spent the next several days trying to round up his remaining troops as they fled back toward Hillsborough. The Virginia General Assembly raised more militia in response to this disaster, and Stevens was assigned to help train them for service. Out of these efforts developed a new Southern Army under the command of Major General Nathanael Greene. Under orders from General

Greene, Stevens spent the remainder of the year engaged in information gathering and logistical planning.

In early 1781, Stevens was charged with escorting Virginia militia forces whose terms were about to expire back home to Virginia. Meanwhile, he was also placed in command of British POWS captured at the Battle of Cowpens and assigned to escort them to an internment camp in Charlottesville. On the way there, in North Carolina, Stevens intercepted Brigadier General Daniel Morgan and spent a few days assisting him with moving supplies across the Yadkin River near Salisbury. After finishing his assignment in Virginia, Stevens rejoined Greene's force and took command of one of his militia brigades; Brigadier General Robert Lawson commanded the other. On March 15, 1781, Greene moved his army near Guilford Courthouse in an attempt to draw Lord Cornwallis into

Brigadier General Edward Stevens served under Major General Horatio Gates (*shown here*) at the disastrous Battle of Camden on August 16, 1780. *New York Public Library.*

battle. Cornwallis took the bait, and both sides formed battle lines. In an attempt to avoid a repeat of the Camden disaster, Stevens posted guards behind his Virginia militia lines with instructions to shoot any militiamen who attempted to flee. In the ensuing battle, the Virginia militia did hold its ground and fight, even though its North Carolina counterparts quickly gave way. The Virginia force started to pull back only after Stevens was shot in the thigh, forcing his removal from the battlefield. Ultimately, Governor Thomas Jefferson, Major General Nathanael Greene and even the British were all complimentary of the extraordinary heroism demonstrated by Stevens and his men. For Stevens, that went a long way toward removing the stigma he endured following the terrible loss at Camden.

Fortunately for Stevens, the musket ball he took in the thigh turned out to be only a flesh wound. He therefore spent the next few weeks actively planning his return to service while in recovery. In June 1781, he happened to be in Charlottesville when, as part of the wider British invasion of Virginia, dragoons commanded by Lieutenant Colonel Banastre Tarleton attempted to capture Governor Jefferson and the rest of the Virginia General Assembly,

The Battle of Camden was a humiliating experience for General Stevens, which strengthened his resolve to redeem himself in later battles. *New York Public Library.*

which was temporarily meeting there. However, forewarned by patriot militia officer Jack Jouett, Jefferson and most of the legislators were able to evade British capture. Meanwhile, dressed in civilian attire and atop a plain horse, Stevens rode by Tarleton and his men completely unnoticed and was also able to make a successful escape. The following month, he assumed command of a new militia unit under the Marquis de Lafayette and was stationed at Malvern Hill near Richmond. He was not directly involved in the Battles of Spencer's Ordinary or Green Spring, but by mid-September, he was encamped with the growing Allied forces in Williamsburg. On September 28, the Allied Army moved toward Yorktown, where Stevens's brigade formed part of the reserve stationed along the trenches facing the besieged British. As only portions of General Weedon's militia forces in Gloucester saw any combat during the siege, Stevens's force assisted the army primarily in support roles. The following year, Stevens was assigned by Governor Benjamin Harrison to command garrisoned troops at Yorktown and, later, others at Fort Pitt, but due to intervening factors, neither assignment actually materialized. Stevens's military career was, therefore, effectively concluded.

Following the war, Stevens began to pivot toward political pursuits. Even during the conflict, he served in the Virginia Senate in 1776 and again from 1779 onward, as this did not interfere with his military activities. As a state senator, he represented Culpeper, Orange and Spotsylvania Counties and remained in office until 1790. In March 1792, Stevens was appointed by President Washington to serve as an excise inspector. Meanwhile, he was an active property owner and church benefactor in his later years. Stevens passed away on August 17, 1820, and was buried in the Masonic Cemetery in Culpeper. The town of Stevensburg in Culpeper County is named in his honor. There is also a monument honoring Stevens on the Guilford Courthouse battlefield.

Chapter 24

LIEUTENANT COLONEL ST. GEORGE TUCKER (1752–1827)

St. George Tucker was one of the most accomplished jurists and legal scholars in the early United States. Over the course of his long career, he sat on three different courts and was also a distinguished educator and scholar. In addition, Tucker was a respected soldier who played a pivotal role during the Siege of Yorktown. Born near Port Royal, Bermuda, on July 10, 1752, he descended from a family that had been prominent on that island since the 1640s. Tucker's parents were Colonel Henry Tucker, a prosperous merchant, and Anne Butterfield, the daughter of a chief justice of Bermuda. Named for his great-grandfather, Tucker attended grammar school in Bermuda from 1768 to 1770 and then set sail for America in 1771 to attend The College of William & Mary. Tucker originally intended to study law at the Inns of Court in London, but a financial downturn made the Virginia College the more affordable option. At William & Mary, Tucker frequented the most elite social circles, rubbing elbows with such families as the Nelsons and the Fairfaxes. Short of funds, Tucker left the College in 1772 to engage in a legal apprenticeship with the eminent lawyer George Wythe in Williamsburg. He was admitted to the Virginia Bar on April 4, 1774.

Although Tucker originally intended to practice law, a series of circumstances led him to take part in a prosperous family-run smuggling business. In that capacity, he returned to Bermuda and used his Virginia contacts to negotiate contracts for smuggled goods, including salt, sugar, rice, tobacco and munitions. Tucker and his family prospered by transporting these items all over the Americas, the Caribbean and Europe between 1776 and 1779. Back in Williamsburg, in January 1777, he met Frances Bland Randolph, the wealthy widow of John Randolph, who had three young children. Her youngest son, John Randolph, would go on to become a U.S. congressman, U.S. senator and U.S. ambassador to Russia. Frances descended from the distinguished Bland family, and her brother Theodorick Bland was close friends with Tucker. The pair married in September 1778 and had several children together. The couple also circulated within Virginia's most elite social circles and owned multiple homes, including the 1,300 acre Matoax estate in Chesterfield County and the 800-acre Bizarre estate, located in Cumberland County.

Lieutenant Colonel St. George Tucker.
New York Public Library.

In the spring of 1779, Tucker desired to pursue military service and joined the militia. Although he initially enlisted as a private, his political connections quickly allowed him to secure a major's commission; he served in Colonel Beverley Randolph's regiment under Brigadier General Robert Lawson. Tucker later fought at the Battle of Guilford Courthouse on March 15, 1781, where he was wounded in action, taking a bayonet in the leg while trying to stop a fleeing soldier. However, Tucker managed to recover and secured a promotion to lieutenant colonel in command of a volunteer regiment. During this time, he was also busy shuffling his young family between their various properties in an attempt to keep them away from the advancing British. In July 1781, Tucker reunited with his brother Thomas, a Continental Army surgeon who had been recently released from British captivity in a prisoner exchange. The brothers then returned to Williamsburg, where Tucker was assigned to the Marquis de Lafayette's command. Fluent in French, he enjoyed mingling with French officers and even became close friends with the Vicomte de Ponteves Gien, who was a French Navy captain.

In September 1781, Tucker was on hand in Williamsburg to help welcome General Washington to the former colonial capital. Washington immediately recognized him from their prewar days. Shortly before the Siege of Yorktown,

Colonel Tucker's alma mater, The College of William & Mary. *New York Public Library.*

Tucker was appointed by Brigadier General Thomas Nelson to serve on his staff as a French interpreter. This undoubtedly pleased Tucker immensely, as this assignment allowed him to interact with the highest levels of Allied command. As the operations at Yorktown progressed, he was wounded a second time when an artillery shell exploded near him, resulting in a minor wound to his nose. Notwithstanding Tucker's administrative service, his greatest contribution to the Yorktown Campaign was the detailed journal he maintained about the siege, providing important insights about everything he was observing around him. It is a rich source of information still utilized by Revolutionary War scholars today.

Following the war, Tucker served on the Council of State from January to May 1782. Later that year, he was appointed to William & Mary's Board of Visitors, and he went on to serve as the College's rector from 1789 to 1790. Rather reluctantly, Tucker also returned to the field of law, where he practiced across several central Virginia counties. He would have preferred the life of a planter, but postwar financial realities necessitated the steadier income stream provided by legal work. In March 1783, he was named commonwealth's attorney for Chesterfield County. Virginia's legal community soon took notice of this budding lawyer, and further professional opportunities soon followed. In 1786, he served alongside James Madison and Edmund Randolph as a delegate to the Annapolis Convention, a multistate assembly that explored the idea of reversing the protectionist trade barriers that each participating state had established. Then, in 1789, Tucker was appointed to serve as a district court judge, a distinction that reflected his growing influence in the state's legal community. He was also active during this time in helping rewrite Virginia's laws, which were in a state of transition following the American Revolution. However, as Tucker's professional career was beginning to blossom, personal tragedy struck when his wife, Frances, died following childbirth. This unfortunate event prompted him to move to Williamsburg with his young family, where he would marry Lelia Skipwith Carter, daughter of Sir Peyton Skipwith, a few years later. A young widow who had once been a teacher of Tucker's daughter Frances, Lelia brought two of her own children into the marriage. The family lived in a residence now known as the Tucker House in Williamsburg.

Another important outcome of Tucker's return to Williamsburg was his increased interaction with The College of William & Mary. While Tucker was serving as rector in 1790, his old mentor George Wythe resigned his professorship, and Tucker was appointed to succeed him, earning an honorary doctorate in civil law in the process. As opposed to the apprentice model, which was how he studied law, Tucker became an early advocate for a more formal and structured approach to legal education. He therefore adopted William Blackstone's *Commentaries on the Laws of England* as his standard course text. The College also began offering its first bachelor of law (LLB) degree during Tucker's professorship. Students began to come from other states and even countries to have the opportunity to study under him. He generally taught out of his house so he could have easy access to his vast collection of legal books. Tucker also remained active in his professional legal work and even submitted a plan to

Colonel Tucker served under the Marquis de Lafayette (*shown here*) prior to the Siege at Yorktown. *New York Public Library.*

The St. George Tucker House in Williamsburg. *Library of Congress.*

the Virginia General Assembly in 1795 for the gradual abolition of slavery in Virginia, which was never acted on. He consequently continued with his faculty duties at William & Mary. However, when the College began requiring courses be taught on campus, along with implementing other policies that Tucker deemed unreasonable, he resigned his position in March 1804 to return to full-time legal work.

Owing to a vacancy brought about by Justice Edmund Pendleton's death in October 1803, Tucker was appointed to the state's Supreme Court of Appeals (now known as the Virginia Supreme Court) in January 1804. In that capacity, he helped preside over a number of important cases before resigning in March 1811. The subsequent War of 1812 proved to be a difficult period for Tucker, as he had several relatives fighting on opposing sides of the conflict. Nevertheless, he continued in his legal work, and a short time later, President James Madison nominated him to serve on the U.S. District Court in Virginia. Although he was initially reluctant to serve due to his advancing age and other considerations, Tucker eventually accepted the post and was confirmed by the U.S. Senate on January 19, 1813. In this role, he heard cases twice a year and worked with Chief Justice John Marshall on the U.S. Circuit Court when it met in Richmond. The district was later split into eastern and western halves, and Tucker consequently joined the U.S. District Court for the Eastern District of Virginia in 1819.

However, his advancing age and mounting health problems eventually made it too difficult for him to serve, and Tucker resigned the post on June 30, 1825. In retirement, Tucker and his wife divided their time between Williamsburg and the Edgewood Estate in Nelson County that belonged to his stepdaughter Mary Carter Cabell. Two years later, he had a stroke while staying at Edgewood and died on November 10, 1827. Tucker was buried in Nelson County. His brother Thomas Tudor Tucker went on to become a U.S. congressman who also served as U.S. treasurer from 1801 to 1828. Another brother, Henry Tucker, served as president of the Council of Bermuda and also, occasionally, as acting governor. Moreover, several of Tucker's descendants went on to distinguished careers in the political, military and legal realms.

Chapter 25

COLONEL SAMUEL VANCE
(CIRCA 1734–1807)

Relatively little is known about Samuel Vance's early years. It is believed that he was born in approximately 1734 in County Antrim, Ireland, and was among Augusta County's early settlers. Vance entered the historical record in 1763, when he married Sarah Bird; a couple of years later, he established a plantation near Mountain Grove in modern-day Bath County. They would reside there for over forty years and raise a family of eight children. Vance served in the local militia during this period, holding the rank of lieutenant by May 1774. Later that year, he served under Colonel Andrew Lewis and saw action at the Battle of Point Pleasant, where on October 10 they fought Indians under the command of the notable Shawnee Chief Cornstalk. Vance was wounded during this engagement but later recovered enough to take part in the growing rebellion against the British. In 1777, he commanded a local militia company that was tasked with guarding the area around Clover Lick Fort against Indians. By 1778, he had become a noted civic and military leader in Augusta County, serving as a militia captain as well as a justice of the local court. During the war's later stages, Vance progressed to the rank of colonel, commanding Augusta and Rockingham County militia forces during the Siege of Yorktown. On October 1, 1781, Vance and his forces were reportedly encamped four miles below Williamsburg, with militia reinforcements joining them. Following the siege, Vance's regiment helped guard surrendered British forces as they were marched to captivity in Winchester, Virginia.

Following the surrender at Yorktown, Colonel Samuel Vance and his troops helped guard British prisoners as they were marched to captivity. *Bicast Inc., Walter Miller.*

After the war, Vance resumed his public leadership roles in Augusta County, serving as a justice and commissioner of the tax. However, Vance and his colleagues were often displeased by the long-distance travel required to successfully perform their duties. Thus, by the late 1780s, he had joined a movement to create a new locality, which culminated in 1790 with the establishment of Bath County. In this new jurisdiction, Vance served as one of the first justices and as the county coroner, holding these offices for over a decade. Vance performed a final civic role in 1794, when he was appointed to a commission to study the best route for the planned James River and Kanawha Turnpike. As someone who had traveled through that area extensively to perform both his civic and military duties, Vance was an excellent choice for such an assignment. He passed away in September 1807, followed by his widow, Sarah, in 1815. They were both likely buried in the vicinity of Mountain Grove, but the exact location of their grave sites remains unknown.

Chapter 26

LIEUTENANT COLONEL JOHN WEBB

(1747–1826)

John Webb was born on January 18, 1747, in Essex County. His parents, James William Webb and Mary Edmondson, had long been situated in that part of Virginia. On reaching adulthood, he married Amy Booker of Essex County's South Farnham Parish on February 20, 1772, and he went on to have approximately twelve children with her. As the American Revolution commenced, Webb rallied quickly to the patriot cause and joined the growing Continental Army. By March 1776, he was serving as a captain in the Seventh Virginia Regiment, which was originally commanded by Colonel Alexander McClanahan, who served in Brigadier General William Woodford's brigade. The Seventh Virginia joined General Washington's main army at Morristown in January 1777 and suffered heavy losses at the Battle of Brandywine, which was fought in September that year.

Webb was promoted to major on January 26, 1778, and was encamped at Valley Forge until that March, when he and other officers from the Seventh Virginia were sent back home on furlough to assist with recruiting. In July, Webb returned to the main army, which was encamped at White Plains, New York. By September 1778, the Seventh Virginia had been renamed the Fifth Virginia Regiment, and he was transferred to that new unit. A few months later, Webb was the sole field officer present with the regiment, which, Baron von Steuben noted in his May 25, 1779 inspector general report, was in a great state of disrepair. Nevertheless, Webb was promoted to lieutenant colonel on July 4, 1779, and continued with the unit until it was combined with the First Virginia Regiment and sent south. Many of its soldiers and officers were later captured following the Siege of Charleston in May 1780. It is unclear whether Webb was with the regiment during that time, but he was listed as supernumerary, and he had officially retired from the Fifth Virginia as of February 12, 1781.

As 1781 progressed, Webb transitioned to militia service to help repel the growing British threat in Virginia. Serving under Brigadier General George Weedon, he commanded a "partizan legion" of four hundred men in September 1781, operating in conjunction with the rest of General Weedon's forces in Gloucester County. As the Yorktown Campaign progressed, Webb's force was reorganized, and to his command was added a fifty-man "corps of horse" that coordinated closely with French troops in the area. By September 17, Webb's forces were stationed near Ware Church in Gloucester, only about four miles from the British Army lines. Suspecting enemy activity, Weedon ordered Webb and his command even closer to enemy lines, sending them to a position near Abington Church on September 22. During this time, they were constantly on the move, keeping a close watch on the enemy lines for any sign of movement. By early October, Webb's force had also provided support to foraging parties that came perilously close to British lines. On October 3, Webb's cavalry, working in conjunction with the Duc de Lauzun's French hussars, encountered British cavalry under Lieutenant Colonel Banastre Tarleton near Gloucester Point, and they exchanged sporadic gunfire. Certain wartime reports that Webb's cavalry fled on first contact

Baron von Steuben (*shown here*) noted that Lieutenant Colonel John Webb's regiment was in a state of disrepair during a 1779 inspection. *New York Public Library.*

Colonel Webb served with the Duc de Lauzun (*shown here*) during the Battle of the Hook in Gloucester. *New York Public Library.*

with the British have been questioned by modern historians, as they would have been riding side by side with experienced French forces. Regardless, so began the Battle of the Hook, in which Webb and his forces played a vital part.

Following the British surrender at Yorktown, Webb returned home and prepared his family for a new chapter. On January 1, 1782, he purchased 316 acres of land in Granville County, North Carolina, from his brother-in-law, and he moved there shortly thereafter. Once established in North Carolina, Webb severed his ties with the Anglican Church and began to associate with the Grassy Creek Presbyterian Church, where he served as an elder. By all accounts, he spent the next several years living a quiet life as a planter. In 1822, Webb was one of the founders of a new congregation called Spring Grove Church, which was located closer to his home. He passed away on August 26, 1826, and when his will was probated that November, he was found to have owned twenty-two enslaved persons. Webb was buried at the Oak Hill Church cemetery in Granville County.

Chapter 27

BRIGADIER GENERAL GEORGE WEEDON
(1734-1793)

George Weedon played a significant role during the Siege of Yorktown, which served for him as the culmination of a long and distinguished Revolutionary War career. As a former Continental Army brigadier general, Weedon was among the most experienced of the Virginia militia commanders who served at Yorktown, helping effectively trap the British forces that were stationed in Gloucester. He was born in 1734 in Westmoreland County and was a son of George and Sarah Gray Weedon. The elder George passed away a few months before his son's birth. Weedon otherwise had a childhood typical of the planter class, hunting and fishing in and around his family's tobacco plantations. Sometime prior to 1743, Sarah Weedon remarried. Thus, in the years that followed, Weedon was raised in part by his stepfather, William Strother. He had his first taste of military service during the French and Indian War, receiving an ensign's commission on September 14, 1755, in return for his work recruiting soldiers for the unit's commander, George Washington. Although most of his wartime service consisted of garrison duty, Weedon earned promotions to lieutenant in 1757 and captain in 1762. During this time, he also met future Revolutionary War hero Hugh Mercer, with whom he became close friends.

Following the war, Weedon moved to Fredericksburg and married Catherine "Kitty" Gordon, who was the daughter of a successful tavern owner. Shortly thereafter, Weedon took over operation of the tavern, which became a popular meeting place for the Virginia elite. Even such notables as

George Washington and Thomas Jefferson occasionally visited the establishment. The tavern provided Weedon, always interested in social advancement, with a golden opportunity to enhance his community standing. Accordingly, he was appointed an officer in the Spotsylvania County militia in 1764. Along with the tavern, Weedon engaged in other enterprises with fellow Fredericksburg resident Hugh Mercer and became quite successful. The pair also developed familial ties following Mercer's marriage to Catherine's sister, Isabela Gordon. Two of Mercer's children were named after Weedon. In the late 1760s, Weedon went into the meat-selling business, engaging in a partnership with Charles Washington, a brother of George Washington. Weedon, strongly interested in horses and horse racing, also introduced subscription racing to the area and was instrumental in establishing the Fredericksburg Jockey Club, whose meetings were held at his tavern.

Brigadier General George Weedon. *New York Public Library.*

By all accounts, Weedon was an early and zealous supporter of the patriot cause, and his tavern became an important meeting place for revolutionary discussion and activity. Moreover, in late 1774, Weedon joined a militia unit known as the Spotsylvania Independent Company to help protect the area from attack. After the war commenced, he rented out his tavern and followed his friend Hugh Mercer into the Continental Army. In January 1776, Weedon was elected lieutenant colonel of the Third Virginia Regiment, while Mercer was elected colonel. After Mercer's promotion to brigadier general that August, Weedon advanced to colonel and commanding officer of the Third Virginia. He spent much of this time serving in Williamsburg and other parts of Virginia. According to legend, because Weedon often distributed punch to his regiment in gourds, his troops fondly referred to him as Joe Gourd. By September 1776, he was actively engaged in the New York Campaign, and he saw action at the Battle of Harlem Heights. That December, Weedon and his regiment fought at the Battle of Trenton and had the honor of being among the first troops to charge against the Hessians.

Two officers in his regiment, Captain William Washington and Lieutenant James Monroe, were wounded in the fighting. Although stricken with the flu, Weedon was granted the additional honor, along with his regiment, of escorting the captured Hessian troops to Philadelphia for processing and confinement. Because of this assignment, Weedon missed the Battle of Princeton on January 3, 1777. Nevertheless, he kept close tabs on battlefield developments and was devastated by the death of his close friend and family member Brigadier General Hugh Mercer. Mercer's widow and her five children would go on to live with Weedon and his wife.

A short time later, Weedon was appointed as interim adjutant general, succeeding Colonel Joseph Reed. Though he preferred field command, Weedon undertook the various administrative responsibilities of the position until a permanent replacement was appointed. Then, on February 21, 1777, he was promoted to brigadier general by act of the Continental Congress. Weedon was given seniority over another recently promoted brigadier general and fellow Virginian, William Woodford, which proved awkward, as Woodford had outranked Weedon as early as the French and Indian War. The rank dispute led to tense relations between the old friends. Following a short official trip to Philadelphia to visit wounded soldiers, Weedon went on a short furlough and returned to Fredericksburg. In between spending time with family and friends, he occupied himself with recruiting new troops and promoting inoculations for the army. By May, he was back in camp with the Continental Army at Morristown, taking command of a brigade in Major General Nathanael Greene's division. That September, Weedon fought at the Battle of Brandywine, earning praise by helping prevent a flanking maneuver by the British. The following month, he also saw action at the Battle of Germantown, and while he was pleased to see heavy British casualties during the fight, Weedon was frustrated about what he considered to be a second missed opportunity for victory following the defeat at Brandywine.

General Weedon was a close friend and family member of Brigadier General Hugh Mercer. *New York Public Library.*

Weedon and his brigade were among those who encamped at Valley Forge, and during that time, he attended to the typical challenges of enforcing discipline, procuring supplies and recruiting new troops. By early 1778, Weedon's troubles had continued to expand as he was embroiled in disputes over seniority and rank. For one, he opposed the practice of giving so many foreign-born offers commissions as general officers. Moreover, he was upset that Congress had reconsidered General Woodford's seniority status and decided to make him senior to Weedon and other brigadier generals. Following a furlough in Fredericksburg, Weedon returned to Valley Forge in May and fretted over his fate. He informed congressional allies that he was considering resignation from the army, but Congress did not act, leaving Weedon in a state of limbo. When a compromise was eventually offered to Weedon in an attempt to resolve the dispute, he deemed it unsatisfactory and decided to leave active service. Congress therefore allowed him to retire and retain his rank. Consequently, Weedon returned to Fredericksburg in September 1778, sick with gout and stress over this recent predicament.

As a newly minted civilian, Weedon enjoyed the benefits of home life—most notably having the opportunity to be a parent to the Mercer children. However, he also missed army life and fretted over his legacy, fearing that fellow Virginians would brand him a quitter. In the following months, Weedon monitored the war's progress from afar and maintained a regular correspondence with Continental Army officers such as General Greene and Colonel Walter Stewart. He also began advocating for Virginia's defense with various state officials. In the closing months of 1779, Weedon began to lobby for a return to active service, either with the Northern Army or in some other capacity. Congress eventually restored him to service and assigned him to the Southern Army, but by June 1780, he still had no specific operational command. Weedon therefore occupied himself with helping recruit new troops in the Fredericksburg area. However, following British General Leslie's Virginia raid in October 1780, Weedon was sent by General Muhlenberg to Richmond to recruit more troops and organize new battalions. The following month, Weedon marched to Williamsburg with nearly one thousand troops and did his best to predict future British movements. He came to prefer service in Virginia as opposed to elsewhere in the southern theater and spent the next several weeks shuttling between Richmond and Fredericksburg. Meanwhile, Mrs. Weedon entertained General Greene and his staff as they passed through Fredericksburg in Greene's new capacity as commander in chief of the Southern Army.

By January 1781, Weedon was once again active in the field, trying to organize militia forces to help repel Benedict Arnold's Virginia invasion. Specifically, his goal was to ensure that Northern Virginia was prepared in case Arnold attempted to attack that area. After organizing troops and equipment, Weedon marched to Williamsburg in March with about seven hundred men. He spent the next few weeks engaged in reconnaissance as well as consultation with the new area commander, the Marquis de Lafayette. Then, in late March, Weedon was assigned command of a Virginia militia brigade situated north of the James River. For the next several weeks, he also remained busy arranging for the defense of sections of Tidewater Virginia and tending to matters of prisoner exchange. During British Major General William Phillips's invasion of Virginia in April 1781, Weedon was also active in preparing defenses in Fredericksburg and the Northern Neck for potential British attack. While this was important work, Weedon worried about being permanently cast in behind-the-scenes support roles and yearned to be back on the front lines. An opportunity to return to the field materialized in early September, when Virginia militia forces were mobilized to encamp at Gloucester in response to Lord Cornwallis's operations in Yorktown. To Weedon's chagrin, Governor Thomas Nelson initially favored Colonel James Innes to lead this militia force. However, following an intervention from the Marquis de Lafayette, the command was eventually offered to Weedon, who eagerly accepted.

General Weedon served under Major General Peter Muhlenberg in late 1780. *New York Public Library.*

On reaching Gloucester, Weedon came to find a force of about 1,500 militia, though only about 1,200 were actually present at any given time. They hailed from counties mostly north of the Pamunkey River, and like other militia, many of them lacked arms and ammunition. Further complicating matters for Weedon, General Washington assigned the Duc de Lauzun and his French forces to Gloucester on September 20 in order to help shore up the militia units in the area. The French Legion ended up numbering about 300 cavalry and 300 infantry. Though neither was

General Weedon and the Duc de Lauzun confer to gather intelligence prior to the Battle of the Hook in this painting by David Wagner. *Gloucester Museum of History.*

supposed to command the other, the arrangement resulted in a tense working relationship between Lauzun and Weedon, who would have preferred for the French forces to be stationed elsewhere. Nevertheless, Weedon persisted in his duty and spent the balance of September organizing his force and reconnoitering the British positions. Among his senior officers were Colonel James Innes, who commanded an "advanced brigade"; Lieutenant Colonel John Webb, who commanded a cavalry formation; and Colonels John Page and William Griffin, who commanded militia regiments. Since Gloucester Point served as an obvious possible escape route for the British, General Washington sent further French reinforcements there in early October. They were led by the Marquis de Choisy, who as a major general became the senior officer in the area, commanding both Weedon's and Lauzun's forces. Thereafter, the Allied forces in Gloucester numbered some 3,000 troops total.

In the days that followed, Weedon maintained a frenzied pace, trying to secure provisions, arms and ammunition for his militia forces while supporting Allied operations against the nearby British, including the Battle

Virginia Militia Commanders at Yorktown

General George Washington was a regular visitor to Brigadier General George Weedon's tavern in Fredericksburg. *New York Public Library.*

of the Hook on October 3. He was hampered by a lack of wagons, which prevented him from advancing his main body of troops in force. During this time, Weedon was also charged with helping prevent a possible British escape out of Yorktown by rounding up boats and having men on standby to fell trees to obstruct roads, if necessary. Though this work was vital, Weedon felt that he was yet again being relegated to support roles. Following the British surrender on October 19, he was also disturbed that only a small portion of his forces, those commanded by Lieutenant Colonel John Francis Mercer, were allowed by General Choisy to participate alongside the French in the surrender ceremony at Gloucester Point. Therefore, it is likely that Weedon was not present for that historical event. Nevertheless, he joined his comrades in arms in celebrating the Allied success that brought them a major step closer to total victory.

As the war began to wind down, Weedon was able to return to Fredericksburg for a well-deserved rest. Although he'd had his share of disputes and disagreements with fellow officers, Weedon ended his wartime service with universal respect: many realized that few others had done more to serve and protect Virginia. With the dawn of peace, Weedon formally resigned his commission on July 11, 1783, and he held a now legendary Peace Ball at his tavern that November. Unlike many of his fellow officers, Weedon did not pursue public office or political appointment in the Confederation government, though he did briefly entertain the idea of seeking out a federal military position. In the fall of 1783, Weedon was a founder of the Virginia Society of the Cincinnati, and he served as one of its first presidents. The Society enabled Weedon to maintain ties with his brother officers and reflect on wartime experiences. As the 1780s progressed, he also served on the Fredericksburg City Council and was even mayor for a single term in 1785. Moreover, Weedon was a respected community leader in other areas, helping establish a new St. George's Episcopal Church as well as a new school, known as the Fredericksburg Academy. He served as an active Freemason as well. On the domestic front, with no children of their own, Weedon and his wife, Kitty, continued to help raise the Mercer children and provide for them to the best of their ability. They also enjoyed the company of friends and entertained George Washington and other Revolutionary War notables whenever they passed through Fredericksburg.

Although he owned other properties, Weedon immersed himself in building a new home in Fredericksburg, known as the Sentry Box, and he and his family moved there around 1786. Living postwar life to its fullest, he also began to overindulge in eating, drinking and gambling. Consequently, and in combination with the lingering effects of gout, his health began to decline around 1792. Weedon passed away on December 23, 1793; Kitty passed away four years later. They are both buried in the Masonic Cemetery in Fredericksburg.

Chapter 28

LIEUTENANT COLONEL GEORGE WEST
(CIRCA 1733–1786)

The Wests are one of Virginia's oldest and most prestigious historical families, dating to the early days of the Jamestown Colony. Its immigrant ancestor Colonel John West first arrived in Virginia in 1618, one of four brothers to seek fortune in the New World. A graduate of Magdalene College at Oxford and a son of Sir Thomas West (Second Baron De La Warr) and Lady Anne Knollys (a cousin of Queen Elizabeth I), he went on to reside in York County and, later, West Point, and serve as Virginia's acting governor from 1635 to 1637. Some of his descendants later settled in northern Virginia and achieved prominence in Fairfax County and its surrounding areas. For instance, a great-great-grandson, Hugh West, was instrumental in founding the City of Alexandria in 1749. At the time, area residents deemed riverfront property that he owned desirable for the development of a town, and a young George Washington even helped survey the land. Following Alexandria's establishment, Hugh West went on to serve as a town trustee and church vestryman before passing away in 1754. He was buried in the Pohick Episcopal Church Cemetery in the Lorton section of Fairfax County.

Relatively little is known about the life of his son, George West. Born in approximately 1733, he most likely grew up in Fairfax County and found work as a surveyor in his early years. As a young adult, he may have also settled in neighboring Loudoun County, which was founded in 1757. At the dawn of the American Revolution, West was an ardent proponent of the patriot cause and therefore established himself as a leader in the Loudoun

County militia, which by 1775 was Virginia's largest. Appointed a captain in May 1777, he rose quickly through the ranks, gaining promotions to major in May 1778 and lieutenant colonel in November 1780. By July 1781, West commanded a militia regiment, and to support the gathering forces at Yorktown, he marched it from Leesburg to Gloucester by way of Falmouth, Fredericksburg and Bowling Green. In Gloucester, he served in Brigadier General George Weedon's brigade. At one point during the siege, West and his regiment were ordered to assault the enemy works at Gloucester Point. However, the position was deemed too well fortified, so the operation was later called off. Following the British surrender at Yorktown, West's regiment was assigned to escort prisoners back to northern Virginia, where they would be sent on to camps in Winchester, Virginia; Frederick, Maryland; or Carlisle, Pennsylvania. Perhaps in recognition of his honorable service during the Yorktown Campaign, West was promoted to full colonel in March 1782. He passed away in 1786 and, like his father, was buried in the Pohick Episcopal Church Cemetery in Lorton.

Lieutenant Colonel George West's ancestor Thomas West, Third Baron De La Warr. *New York Public Library.*

Appendix A

Chronology of the Siege of Yorktown

Adapted from William W. Reynolds's article "The Virginia Militia at the Siege of Yorktown" in *Military Collector & Historian* 67, no. 2 (Summer 2025): 171.

Date	Summary of Events
September 28	Allied Army marched twelve miles from Williamsburg to Yorktown
September 29	Allied commanders reconnoitered British lines. During the night, British evacuated their outer works.
September 30	Allied Army occupied British outer works and began reversing their fronts.
October 1–2	Allied Army prepared fascines and gabions in preparation for siege and began hauling siege artillery from Trebell's Landing on James River to Yorktown.
October 3	Battle of the Hook in Gloucester County resulted in British forces there confined to Gloucester Point. Siege preparations continued in Yorktown.
October 4–5	Siege preparations and hauling of siege artillery continued.

Appendix A

October 6	During the night, Allied Army excavated trench of the second parallel.
October 7–8	Allies constructed batteries and redoubts and positioned siege artillery.
October 9	Allies opened fire on British from first parallel.
October 10	Firing continued day and night.
October 11	Firing continued day and night. Allies excavated trench of the second parallel.
October 12	Firing continued day and night from first parallel. Allies began to construct batteries and redoubts of second parallel.
October 13	Firing continued day and night from first parallel. Allied continued to construct batteries and redoubts of second parallel.
October 14	Firing continued day and night from first parallel. Allies stormed and took Redoubts 9 and 10 while diversionary attack was made on the British works at Gloucester Point. Redoubts 9 and 10 reconfigured to face British lines and trench of second parallel extended to redoubts.
October 15	Firing continued from first parallel. Firing began from second parallel.
October 16	Firing continued.
October 17	Cornwallis requested a parley and proposed terms of surrender.
October 18	Terms of surrender negotiated.
October 19	Articles of Capitulation signed. British Army surrendered to Allied Army at 1400 in front of Yorktown, and at 1500 near Gloucester Point.
October 21	Virginia militia forces commanded by Brigadier General Robert Lawson begin marching British prisoners of war to Winchester, Virginia, and Frederick, Maryland.

Appendix B

Partial List of Virginia Militia Units Present at the Siege of Yorktown

As noted in J.T. McAllister's *Virginia Militia in the Revolutionary War*.

Albemarle County

Captain Benjamin Harris's Company

Amelia County

Captain Lewis Ford's Company

Augusta County

Captain James Bell's Company
Captain ____ Buchannon's Company
Captain ____ Christian's Company
Captain ____ Dickey's Company
Captain Thomas Hicklin's Company
Captain Francis Long's Company
Captain ____ Trimble's Company

Appendix B

Berkeley County (West Virginia)

Captain ____ Coher's Company

Botetourt County

Captain David May's Company
Captain James Smith's Company

Buckingham County

Captain William Giles's Company
Captain Silas Watkins's Company

Caroline County

Captain ____ Coleman's Company
Captain Creed Haskins's Company

Charlotte County

Captain Andrew Wallace's Company

Chesterfield County

Captain David Patterson's Company

Culpeper County

Captain ____ Berkeley's Company

Appendix B

Fauquier County

Captain James Winn's Company

Fluvanna County

Captain Richard Napper's Company

Frederick County

Captain ____ Bell's Company
Captain Joseph Looney's Company

Halifax County

Captain John Falkner's Company

Hanover County

Captain John Thompson's Company

Henry County

Captain ____ Ruble's Company

Louisa County

Captain Samuel Pettis's Company

Pittsylvania County

Captain Fleming Bates's Company

Captain William Dix's Company
Captain Charles Hutchings's Company
Captain Charles Williams's Company

Powhatan County

Captain Hugh Woodson's Company

Prince Edward County

Captain ____ Bird's Company

Rockbridge County

Captain Charles Campbell's Company
Captain David Gray's Company
Captain William Moore's Company

Rockingham County

Captain Michael Cowger's Company
Captain Richard Rigger's Company
Captain ____ Smith's Company

Spotsylvania County

Captain Francis Coleman's Company
Captain ____ Tankersley's Company

Appendix C

Virginia Militia Casualties at the Siege of Yorktown

Adapted from Adjutant General Edward Hand's original November 1781 returns as listed in Henry P. Johnston's *The Yorktown Campaign and the Surrender of Cornwallis—1781.*

From the Battle of the Hook, October 3, 1781:
   Militia (Lieutenant Colonel John Francis Mercer's Militia Grenadiers): Unknown.

From the investiture of York to the opening of the first parallel, on the evening of October 6, exclusive:
   Militia: Killed, 1 rank and file; wounded, 6 rank and file.

From the opening of the second parallel to October 14, inclusive:
   Militia: Killed, 3 rank and file; wounded, 7 rank and file.

Appendix D

VIRGINIA MILITIA COMMANDERS AT THE SIEGE OF YORKTOWN

Brigadier General Thomas Nelson Jr. (Commanding)

<u>Lawson's Brigade, 750 Troops (Stationed at Yorktown)</u>
Brigadier General Robert Lawson (1748–1805), Prince Edward County
   Colonel Sampson Mathews (circa 1737–1807), Augusta County
   Colonel Beverly Randolph (1754–1797), Henrico County
   Colonel Holt Richeson (1736–circa 1800), King William County
   Lieutenant Colonel Henry Skipwith (1751–1815), Cumberland County

<u>Stevens's Brigade, 750 Troops (Stationed at Yorktown)</u>
Brigadier General Edward Stevens (1745–1820), Culpeper County
   Lieutenant Colonel William Darke (1736–1801), Shepherdstown
   Colonel Elias Edmonds (1756–1800), Fauquier County
   Colonel Thomas Meriwether (1763–1802), Caroline County

<u>Weedon's Brigade, 1,500 Troops (Stationed in Gloucester)</u>
Brigadier General George Weedon (1734–1793), Fredericksburg
   Lieutenant Colonel James Baytop (1754–1822), Gloucester
   Colonel Lewis Burwell (1745–1800), Mecklenburg County
   Colonel James Innes (1754–1798), Williamsburg
   Colonel William Griffin (1742–1793), King and Queen County
   Lieutenant Colonel John Francis Mercer (1759–1821), Stafford County
   Colonel John Page (1743–1808), Gloucester County

Appendix D

Colonel Sir John Peyton (1720–1790), Gloucester County
Colonel Samuel Vance (circa 1734–circa 1807), Augusta County
Lieutenant Colonel John Webb (1740–1826), Essex County
Colonel George West (1732–1786), Loudoun County

Virginia State Troops, 200 Troops (Stationed at Yorktown)
Lieutenant Colonel Charles Dabney (1745–1829), Hanover County

Lewis's Rifle Corps, 250 Troops (Stationed at Yorktown)
Colonel William Lewis (1724–1811), Augusta County

Other/Staff Officers
Lieutenant Colonel William Fontaine (1754–1810), Hanover County
Colonel Reuben Lindsay (1747–1831), Albemarle County
Lieutenant Colonel Thomas Mathews (1742–1812), Norfolk
Colonel William Nelson (1746–1807), Hanover County
Lieutenant Colonel St. George Tucker (1752–1827), Williamsburg

Appendix E

Virginia Militia Commanders at the Siege of Yorktown Who Are Eligible for Representation in the Society of the Cincinnati (Based upon Prior Continental Army Service)

Lieutenant Colonel James Baytop (1754–1822), Gloucester County, ORIGINAL MEMBER

Colonel Charles Dabney (1745–1829), Hanover County, ORIGINAL MEMBER

Lieutenant Colonel William Darke (1736–1801), Shepherdstown

Colonel Elias Edmonds (1756–1800), Fauquier County

Lieutenant Colonel William Fontaine (1754–1810), Hanover County

Colonel James Innes (1754–1798), Williamsburg, ORIGINAL MEMBER

Brigadier General Robert Lawson (1748–1805), Prince Edward County, ORIGINAL MEMBER

Lieutenant Colonel Thomas Mathews (1742–1812), Norfolk, ORIGINAL MEMBER

Lieutenant Colonel John Francis Mercer (1759–1821), Stafford County

Colonel Thomas Meriwether (1763–1802), Caroline County

Colonel William Nelson (1746–1807), Hanover County

Colonel Holt Richeson (1736–circa 1800), King William County

Lieutenant Colonel John Webb (1740–1826), Essex County

Brigadier General George Weedon (1734–1793), Fredericksburg, ORIGINAL MEMBER

Bibliography

Archival Records

Beverley Randolph Executive Papers, 1788–1791, State Records Collection, Library of Virginia, Richmond, Virginia.
Burwell Family Papers, 1745–1997, Wilson Special Collections Library, University of North Carolina, Chapel Hill, North Carolina.
Charles William Dabney Papers, 1715–1945, Wilson Special Collections Library, University of North Carolina, Chapel Hill, North Carolina.
M. Diggs Collection, Herman Hollerith Archives, Mathews Memorial Library, Mathews, Virginia.

Books

Babits, Lawrence, and Joshua Howard. *Long, Obstinate, and Bloody: The Battle of Guilford Courthouse.* University of North Carolina Press, 2009.
Boogher, William F. *Gleanings of Virginia History: An Historical and Genealogical Collection, Largely from Original Sources.* Self-published, 1965.
Buchanan, John. *The Road to Guilford Courthouse: The American Revolution in the Carolinas.* John Wiley & Sons, 1997.
Carson, Jane. *James Innes and His Brothers of the F.H.C.* University of Virginia Press, 1965.
Colket, Meredith B., Jr. *Founders of Early American Families: Emigrants from Europe, 1607–1657.* Founders and Patriots of America: 1985.

BIBLIOGRAPHY

Crozier, William A. *Virginia Heraldica: Being a Registry of Virginia Gentry Entitled to Coat Armor, with Genealogical Notes of the Families.* Genealogical Association, 1908.

Dodson, E. Griffith. *Speakers and Clerks of the Virginia House of Delegates 1776–1955.* Virginia House of Delegates, 1956.

English, Frederick. *General Hugh Mercer: Forgotten Hero of the American Revolution.* Princeton University Press, 1975.

Greene, Jerome. *The Guns of Independence: The Siege of Yorktown, 1781.* Savas Beatie, 2005.

Grossman, Mark. *Encyclopedia of the Continental Congresses.* Vol. 2, *L–Z.* Grey House Publishing, 2015.

Gwathmey, John. *Historical Register of Virginians in the Revolution: Soldiers, Sailors, Marines, 1775–1783.* Dietz Press, 1938.

Hamilton, Phillip. *The Tuckers of Virginia, 1752–1830: The Making and Unmaking of a Revolutionary Family.* University of Virginia Press, 2008.

Hannings, Bud. *American Revolutionary War Leaders: A Biographical Dictionary.* McFarland & Company, 2009.

Harris, Malcolm Hart. *Old New Kent County: Some Account of the Planters, Plantations, and Places in King William County St. John's Parish.* Vol. 2. Self-published, 1977.

Heitman, Francis. *Historical Register of Officers of the Continental Army During the War of the Revolution, April 1775 to December 1783.* Rare Book Shop Publishing, 1914.

Hetzel, Susan Riviere. *Lineage Book: National Society of the Daughters of the American Revolution.* Vol. 16. Daughters of the American Revolution, 1903.

Johnson, Henry P. *The Yorktown Campaign and the Surrender of Cornwallis.* Corner House Publishers, 1975 (reprint of 1881 original).

Kale, Wilford. *Yorktown, Virginia: A Brief History.* The History Press, 2018.

Kemp, Alan. *Yorktown.* Great Battles Series. Almark Publishing, 1976.

Lanciano, Claude, Jr. *Rosewell: Garland of Virginia.* Delmar, 1978.

Lee, Nell Moore. *Patriot Above Profit: A Portrait of Thomas Nelson, Jr., Who Supported the American Revolution with His Purse and Sword.* Rutledge Hill Press, 1988.

Lewis, Elizabeth Dutton. *Revolutionary War Roster, Gloucester County, Virginia.* Gloucester County Historical and Bicentennial Committees, 1976.

Maass, John. *The Road to Yorktown: Jefferson, Lafayette, and the British Invasion of Virginia.* The History Press, 2015.

McAllister, J.T. *Virginia Militia in the Revolutionary War: McAllister's Data.* McAllister Publishing, 1913.

Morrissey, Brendan. *Yorktown 1781: The World Turned Upside Down*. Osprey Publishing, 1997.
Page, Richard Channing Moore. *Genealogy of the Page Family in Virginia: Also, a Condensed Account of the Nelson, Walker, Pendleton, and Randolph Families.* Jenkins & Thomas Printers, 1883.
Peyton, J. Lewis. *History of Augusta County, Virginia.* Samuel M. Vost & Son, 1882.
Price, David. *Rescuing the Revolution: Unsung Patriot Heroes and the Ten Crucial Days of America's War for Independence.* Knox Press, 2016.
Raimo, John. *Biographical Directory of American Colonial and Revolutionary Governors, 1607–1789.* Meckler Books, 1980.
Sinclair, Caroline Baytop. *Gloucester's Past in Pictures*. Donning Company Publishers, 2005.
Stubbs, William, and Elizabeth Stubbs. *A History of Two Virginia Families Transplanted from County Kent, England: Thomas Baytop, Tenterden 1638 and John Catlett, Sittingbourne 1622.* Self-published, 1918.
Tucker, Robert. *The Descendants of William Tucker of Throwleigh, Devon.* Reprint Company Publishers, 1991.
Tyler, Lyon Gardiner. *Encyclopedia of Virginia Biography*. Vol. 1. Lewis Historical Publishing Company, 1915.
Waddell, Joseph Addison. *Annals of Augusta County, Virginia, from 1726 to 1871.* C. Russell Caldwell, Publisher, 1902.
Ward, Harry. *Duty, Honor or County: General George Weedon and the American Revolution.* American Philosophical Society, 1979.
———. *For Virginia and for Independence: Twenty-Eight Revolutionary War Soldiers from the Old Dominion.* McFarland & Company, 2011.
Webb, William J. *Our Webb Kin of Dixie: A Family History.* Self-published, 1940.
White, Frank, Jr. *The Governors of Maryland, 1777–1970.* Twentieth Century Printing Company, 1970.
Wolf, Christopher E. *Ghosts of the Revolutionary War*. Schiffer Publishing, 2010.
Wright, Robert K., Jr. *The Continental Army.* U.S. Army Center for Military History, 1983.

Dissertations and Theses

Biller, John C. "Henry Skipwith of Hors du Monde, Cumberland County, Virginia." Master's thesis, University of Virginia, 1963.
Ryan, Joanne Wood. "Gloucester County, Virginia, in the American Revolution." Master's thesis, The College of William & Mary, 1978.

BIBLIOGRAPHY

Journal Articles

Arthur, Robert. "The Siege of Yorktown—1781." *Military Engineer* 48, no. 326 (November–December 1956): 448–51.

Bonte, Marie Louise Quarles. "Records of the Richeson Family." *William & Mary Quarterly* 26, no. 4 (April 1918): 259–62.

Bruce, Philip, and William Stanard. "Depositions of Continental Soldiers." *Virginia Magazine of History and Biography* 5 (1897): 153–55.

———. "Lindsays of Virginia." *Virginia Magazine of History and Biography* 11 (1903): 101–02.

Dabney, Charles William. "Colonel Charles Dabney of the Revolution: His Service as Soldier and Citizen." *Virginia Magazine of History and Biography* 51, no. 2 (1943): 186–99.

Edmonds, Albert Sydney. "Edmonium, 1741–Oak Spring, 1759: Elias, William and John Edmonds, Pioneers in Fauquier County, Va." *William & Mary Quarterly* 17, no. 2 (April 1937): 292–300.

Handley, Harry. "The Mathews Trading Post." *Journal of the Greenbrier Historical Society* 1, no. 1 (1963): 10.

Harris, J.D. "General Thomas Mathews." *Virginia Law Register* 7, no. 3 (July 1901): 153–58.

Hatch, Charles, Jr. "Gloucester Point in the Siege of Yorktown 1781." *William & Mary Quarterly* 20, no. 2 (April 1940): 265–84.

Herndon, G. Melvin. "George Mathews, Frontier Patriot." *Virginia Magazine of History and Biography* 77, no. 3 (July 1969): 307–28.

Kemper, Charles. "The Valley of Virginia 1765–1782." *Virginia Magazine of History and Biography* 38, no. 3 (July 1930): 235–40.

King, George Harrison Sanford. "Copies of Extant Wills from Counties Whose Records Have Been Destroyed: Will of Colonel Holt Richeson of 'Kentuckie,' King William County, Virginia." *Tyler's Quarterly Genealogical and Historical Magazine* 33 (July 1919): 49–52.

Neville, Gabriel. "William Darke and George Washington in Politics, Business and War." *Magazine of the Jefferson County Historical Society* 84 (2018): 23–38.

Reynolds, William. "The Virginia Militia at the Siege of Yorktown." *Military Collector & Historian* 67, no. 2 (Summer 2015): 168–86.

Riley, Edward. "St. George Tucker's Journal of the Siege of Yorktown, 1781." *William & Mary Quarterly* 5, no. 3 (July 1948): 375–95.

———. "Yorktown During the Revolution: Part I." *Virginia Magazine of History and Biography* 57, no. 1 (January 1949): 22–43.

Sweeny, Lenora Higginbotham. "William Benson and Captain Elias Edmonds' Company of Artillery at Yorktown." *Virginia Magazine of History and Biography* 67, no. 4 (October 1959): 429–31.

Swope, Frances Alderson. "The Mathews Trading Post Ledger, 1771–1779." *Journal of the Greenbrier Historical Society* 4, no. 4 (1984): 20–22.

Wright, John. "Notes on the Siege of Yorktown in 1781 with Special Reference to the Conduct of Siege in the Eighteenth Century." *William & Mary Quarterly* 12, no. 4 (October 1932): 229–50.

Legal, Public and Organizational Reports

Alma Mater of a Nation: A Bicentennial Sampler for the College of William & Mary. College of William & Mary, 1965.

The Bicentennial History of Bath County, Virginia: 1791–1991. Heritage House Publishing, 1991.

Bulletin of the King & Queen County Historical Society of Virginia, no. 5 (July 1958). King & Queen County Historical Society.

Bulletin of the King & Queen County Historical Society of Virginia, no. 15 (July 1963). King & Queen Historical Society.

Catts, Wade, Robert Selig, Lewis Burruss and Kevin Bradley. "No Regular Corps Could Have Maintained Its Ground More Firmly: Site Documentation and Preservation Plan for the Battle of the Hook, October 3, 1781." American Battlefield Protection Program Grant Final Report, South River Heritage Consulting (Newark, Delaware), 2021.

Stephenson, Mary A. "George Wythe House Historical Report, Block 21, Building 4." Colonial Williamsburg Foundation Library Research Report Series, 1483. Colonial Williamsburg Foundation Library, 1990.

Virginia in the American Revolution: An Exhibition by the Society of the Cincinnati. Society of the Cincinnati, 2009.

Letters and General Orders

Baylor, George. "To George Washington from Colonel George Baylor, 26 February 1777." Founders Online, National Archives. https://founders.archives.gov/documents/Washington/03-08-02-0475. Original source: *The Papers of George Washington.* Revolutionary War Series, vol. 8, *6 January 1777–27 March 1777*, edited by Frank E. Grizzard Jr. University Press of Virginia, 1998, 444–45.

BIBLIOGRAPHY

Burwell, Lewis. "To Thomas Jefferson from Lewis Burwell, 15 February 1781." Founders Online, National Archives. https://founders.archives.gov/documents/Jefferson/01-04-02-0773. Original source: *The Papers of Thomas Jefferson*, vol. 4, *1 October 1780–24 February 1781*, edited by Julian P. Boyd. Princeton University Press, 1951, 612–13.

Dickenson, John, and Thomas Dickenson. "To James Madison from Thomas and John Dickenson, [ca. 1 October] 1791." Founders Online, National Archives. https://founders.archives.gov/documents/Madison/01-14-02-0074. Original source: *The Papers of James Madison*, vol. 14, *6 April 1791–16 March 1793*, edited by Robert A. Rutland and Thomas A. Mason. University Press of Virginia, 1983, 77–78.

Fontaine, William. "William Fontaine to Thomas Jefferson, 16 September 1809." Founders Online, National Archives. https://founders.archives.gov/documents/Jefferson/03-01-02-0420. Original source: *The Papers of Thomas Jefferson*, Retirement Series, vol. 1, *4 March 1809 to 15 November 1809*, edited by J. Jefferson Looney. Princeton University Press, 2004, 525–28.

Founders Online, National Archives. "Conveyance of Carlton by Charles L. Bankhead and Ann C. Bankhead to their Trustees, 1 April 1815." https://founders.archives.gov/documents/Jefferson/03-08-02-0312. Original source: *The Papers of Thomas Jefferson*, Retirement Series, vol. 8, *1 October 1814 to 31 August 1815*, edited by J. Jefferson Looney. Princeton University Press, 2011, 394–97.

———. "Enclosure: Election Returns, 24 April 1799." https://founders.archives.gov/documents/Washington/06-04-02-0010-0002. Original source: *The Papers of George Washington*, Retirement Series, vol. 4, *20 April 1799–13 December 1799*, edited by W.W. Abbot. University Press of Virginia, 1999, 16–17.

Gordon, William F. "William F. Gordon to Thomas Jefferson, 22 July 1812." Founders Online, National Archives. https://founders.archives.gov/documents/Jefferson/03-05-02-0210. Original source: *The Papers of Thomas Jefferson*, Retirement Series, vol. 5, *1 May 1812 to 10 March 1813*, edited by J. Jefferson Looney. Princeton University Press, 2008, 269–70.

Jefferson, Thomas. "From Thomas Jefferson to Sampson Mathews and John Bowyer, 31 January 1781." Founders Online, National Archives. https://founders.archives.gov/documents/Jefferson/01-04-02-0594. Original source: *The Papers of Thomas Jefferson*, vol. 4, *1 October 1780–24 February 1781*, edited by Julian P. Boyd. Princeton University Press, 1951, 486.

BIBLIOGRAPHY

Lawson, Robert. "To Thomas Jefferson from Robert Lawson, 11 June 1801." Founders Online, National Archives. https://founders.archives.gov/documents/Jefferson/01-34-02-0249. Original source: *The Papers of Thomas Jefferson*, vol. 34, *1 May–31 July 1801*, edited by Barbara B. Oberg. Princeton University Press, 2007, 307–08.

———. "To Thomas Jefferson from Robert Lawson, 15 February 1781." Founders Online, National Archives. https://founders.archives.gov/documents/Jefferson/01-04-02-0776. Original source: *The Papers of Thomas Jefferson*, vol. 4, *1 October 1780–24 February 1781*, edited by Julian P. Boyd. Princeton University Press, 1951, 616–18.

Mason, David. "To George Washington from Colonel David Mason, 4 April 1777." Founders Online, National Archives. https://founders.archives.gov/documents/Washington/03-09-02-0060. Original source: *The Papers of George Washington*, Revolutionary War Series, vol. 9, *28 March 1777–10 June 1777*, edited by Philander D. Chase. University Press of Virginia, 1999, 61–63.

Mathews, Sampson. "From Sampson Mathews, with Jefferson's Instructions to George Muter, 21 January 1781." Founders Online, National Archives. https://founders.archives.gov/documents/Jefferson/01-04-02-0523. Original source: *The Papers of Thomas Jefferson*, vol. 4, *1 October 1780–24 February 1781*, edited by Julian P. Boyd. Princeton University Press, 1951, 420–21.

———. "To Thomas Jefferson from Sampson Mathews, 13 January 1781." Founders Online, National Archives. https://founders.archives.gov/documents/Jefferson/01-04-02-0432. Original source: *The Papers of Thomas Jefferson*, vol. 4, *1 October 1780–24 February 1781*, edited by Julian P. Boyd. Princeton University Press, 1951, 350.

———. "To Thomas Jefferson from Sampson Mathews, 29 January 1781." Founders Online, National Archives. https://founders.archives.gov/documents/Jefferson/01-04-02-0574. Original source: *The Papers of Thomas Jefferson*, vol. 4, *1 October 1780–24 February 1781*, edited by Julian P. Boyd. Princeton University Press, 1951, p. 473.

Page, John. "To Thomas Jefferson from John Page, [1 February 1781]." Founders Online, National Archives. https://founders.archives.gov/documents/Jefferson/01-04-02-0610. Original source: *The Papers of Thomas Jefferson*, vol. 4, *1 October 1780–24 February 1781*, edited by Julian P. Boyd. Princeton University Press, 1951, 497.

Randolph, Beverley. "From George Washington to Beverley Randolph, 16 May 1789." Founders Online, National Archives. https://founders.

BIBLIOGRAPHY

archives.gov/documents/Washington/05-02-02-0226. Original source: *The Papers of George Washington*, Presidential Series, vol. 2, *1 April 1789–15 June 1789*, edited by Dorothy Twohig. University Press of Virginia, 1987, 308–10.

Richeson, Holt. "From George Washington to Lieutenant Colonel Holt Richeson, 1 July 1778." Founders Online, National Archives. https://founders.archives.gov/documents/Washington/03-16-02-0007. Original source: *The Papers of George Washington*, Revolutionary War Series, vol. 16, *1 July–14 September 1778*, edited by David R. Hoth. University of Virginia Press, 2006, 9–10.

———. "To George Washington from Lieutenant Colonel Holt Richeson, 14 April 1779." Founders Online, National Archives. https://founders.archives.gov/documents/Washington/03-20-02-0065. Original source: *The Papers of George Washington*, Revolutionary War Series, vol. 20, *8 April–31 May 1779*, edited by Edward G. Lengel. University of Virginia Press, 2010, 70–71.

Skipwith, Henry. "Henry Skipwith to Thomas Jefferson, 10 July 1809." Founders Online, National Archives. https://founders.archives.gov/documents/Jefferson/03-01-02-0277. Original source: *The Papers of Thomas Jefferson*, Retirement Series, vol. 1, *4 March 1809 to 15 November 1809*, edited by J. Jefferson Looney. Princeton University Press, 2004, 339.

Stevens, Edward. "To George Washington from Colonel Edward Stevens, 15 May 1777." Founders Online, National Archives. https://founders.archives.gov/documents/Washington/03-09-02-0431. Original source: *The Papers of George Washington*, Revolutionary War Series, vol. 9, *28 March 1777–10 June 1777*, edited by Philander D. Chase. University Press of Virginia, 1999, 435–36.

Tucker, St. George. "St. George Tucker to Thomas Jefferson, 21 October 1809." Founders Online, National Archives. https://founders.archives.gov/documents/Jefferson/03-01-02-0486-0001. Original source: *The Papers of Thomas Jefferson*, Retirement Series, vol. 1, *4 March 1809 to 15 November 1809*, edited by J. Jefferson Looney. Princeton University Press, 2004, 617.

Washington, George. "General Orders, 1 March 1779." Founders Online, National Archives. https://founders.archives.gov/documents/Washington/03-19-02-0320. Original source: *The Papers of George Washington*, Revolutionary War Series, vol. 19, *15 January–7 April 1779*, edited by Philander D. Chase and William M. Ferraro. University of Virginia Press, 2009, 291–92.

BIBLIOGRAPHY

Newspaper Articles

Daily Press. "Sir Peyton Left Historic Mark." May 19, 1996.
———. "Wealthy Burwells Owned a Chunk of Virginia." May 3, 1992.
Keys, Jane Griffith. "Peyton Lineage and Arms." *Baltimore Sun*, June 24, 1906.

Pension Applications

Adcock, John. A. "Pension Application of John A. Adcock S21036." Southern Campaign American Revolution Pension Statements & Rosters. https://revwarapps.org/s21036.pdf.

Baytop, James. "Pension Application of James Baytop S37701." Southern Campaign American Revolution Pension Statements & Rosters. https://revwarapps.org/s37701.pdf.

Bowen, Micajah. "Pension Application of Micajah Bowen S29643." Southern Campaign American Revolution Pension Statements & Rosters. https://revwarapps.org/s29643.pdf.

Breedlove, John. "Pension Application of John Breedlove S2102." Southern Campaign American Revolution Pension Statements & Rosters. https://revwarapps.org/s2102.pdf.

Bridgwater, William. "Pension Application of William Bridgwater S6737." Southern Campaign American Revolution Pension Statements & Rosters. https://revwarapps.org/s6737.pdf.

Brooke, Humphrey. "Pension Application of Humphrey Brooke S6763." Southern Campaign American Revolution Pension Statements & Rosters. https://revwarapps.org/s6763.pdf.

Bruce, Benjamin. "Pension Application of Benjamin Bruce R1362." Southern Campaign American Revolution Pension Statements & Rosters. https://revwarapps.org/r1362.pdf.

Butler, Joseph. "Pension Application of Joseph Butler W3384." Southern Campaign American Revolution Pension Statements & Rosters. https://revwarapps.org/w3384.pdf.

Connelly, John. "Pension Application of John Connelly S30345." Southern Campaign American Revolution Pension Statements & Rosters. https://revwarapps.org/s30345.pdf.

Crooke, John. "Pension Application of John Crooke S30970." Southern Campaign American Revolution Pension Statements & Rosters. https://revwarapps.org/s30970.pdf.

Bibliography

Dunbar, Jonathan. "Pension Application of Jonathan Dunbar S19286." Southern Campaign American Revolution Pension Statements & Rosters. https://revwarapps.org/s19286.pdf.

Edmonds, Elias. "Petition Relating to Elias Edmonds (Edmunds) VAS2004." Southern Campaign American Revolution Pension Statements & Rosters. https://revwarapps.org/VAS2004.pdf.

Elgin, Walter. "Pension Application of Walter Elgin S9548." Southern Campaign American Revolution Pension Statements & Rosters. https://revwarapps.org/s9548.pdf.

Fontaine, William. "W7319." Southern Campaign American Revolution Pension Statements & Rosters. https://revwarapps.org/w7319.pdf.

Gaines, Ambrose. "Pension Application of Ambrose Gaines W224." Southern Campaign American Revolution Pension Statements & Rosters. https://revwarapps.org/w224.pdf.

Gall, George. "Pension Application of George Gall S2569." Southern Campaign American Revolution Pension Statements & Rosters. https://revwarapps.org/s2569.pdf.

Gregory, Samuel. "Pension Application of Samuel Gregory R4297." Southern Campaign American Revolution Pension Statements & Rosters. https://revwarapps.org/r4297.pdf.

Guy, William. "Pension Application of William Guy W17969." Southern Campaign American Revolution Pension Statements & Rosters. https://revwarapps.org/w17969.pdf.

Haggard, David. "Pension Application of David Haggard R4429." Southern Campaign American Revolution Pension Statements & Rosters. https://revwarapps.org/r4429.pdf.

Hendrick, Daniel. "Pension application of Daniel Hendrick S8706." Southern Campaign American Revolution Pension Statements & Rosters. https://revwarapps.org/s8706.pdf.

Hereford, John. "Pension application of John Hereford W1425." Southern Campaign American Revolution Pension Statements & Rosters. https://revwarapps.org/w1425.pdf.

Holcombe, Philemon. "Pension Application of Philemon Holcombe: S4399." Southern Campaign American Revolution Pension Statements & Rosters. https://revwarapps.org/s4399.pdf.

Hudgins, Anthony. "Pension Application of Anthony Hudgen (Hudgins) S10883." Southern Campaign American Revolution Pension Statements & Rosters. https://revwarapps.org/s10883.pdf.

Jamieson, Samuel. "Pension Application of Samuel Jamieson W5112." Southern Campaign American Revolution Pension Statements & Rosters. https://revwarapps.org/w5112.pdf.

Jones, John. "Pension Application of John Jones S31171." Southern Campaign American Revolution Pension Statements & Rosters. https://revwarapps.org/s31171.pdf.

Lewis, William. "Pension Application of William Lewis BLWt1300-400." Southern Campaign American Revolution Pension Statements & Rosters. https://revwarapps.org/blwt1300-400.pdf.

Marshall, Thomas. "Bounty Land Warrant Information Relating to Thomas Marshall VAS494." Southern Campaign American Revolution Pension Statements & Rosters. https://revwarapps.org/VAS494.pdf.

Maupin, Daniel. "Pension Application of Daniel Maupin W556." Southern Campaign American Revolution Pension Statements & Rosters. https://revwarapps.org/w556.pdf.

Michaux, Jacob. "Virginia Documents Pertaining to Jacob Michaux VAS1801." Southern Campaign American Revolution Pension Statements & Rosters. https://revwarapps.org/VAS1801.pdf.

Miner, William. "Pension Application of William Miner (Minor) S11070." Southern Campaign American Revolution Pension Statements & Rosters. https://revwarapps.org/s11070.pdf.

Monroe, John. "Pension Application of John Monroe S31267." Southern Campaign American Revolution Pension Statements & Rosters. https://www.revwarapps.org/s31267.pdf.

Peay, George. "Pension Application of George Peay S3673." Southern Campaign American Revolution Pension Statements & Rosters. https://revwarapps.org/s3673.pdf.

Randolph, Beverley. "Pension Application of Beverley Randolph W4774." Southern Campaign American Revolution Pension Statements & Rosters. https://revwarapps.org/w4774.pdf.

Rice, James Brown. "Pension Application of James Brown Rice R8746." Southern Campaign American Revolution Pension Statements & Rosters. https://revwarapps.org/r8746.pdf.

Roberts, Isaac. "Pension Application of Isaac Roberts S19453." Southern Campaign American Revolution Pension Statements & Rosters. https://revwarapps.org/s19453.pdf.

Simmons, Jehu. "Pension Application of Jehu Simmons S6093." Southern Campaign American Revolution Pension Statements & Rosters. https://revwarapps.org/s6093.pdf.

Stone, Henry. "Pension Application of Henry Stone S6151." Southern Campaign American Revolution Pension Statements & Rosters. https://revwarapps.org/s6151.pdf.

Tach, Jacob. "Pension Application of Jacob Tack (Tach) S7677." Southern Campaign American Revolution Pension Statements & Rosters. https://revwarapps.org/s7677.pdf.

Thomas, Charles. "Pension Application of Charles Thomas S31421." Southern Campaign American Revolution Pension Statements & Rosters. https://revwarapps.org/s31421.pdf.

True, Robert. "Pension Application of Robert True W9526." Southern Campaign American Revolution Pension Statements & Rosters. https://revwarapps.org/w9526.pdf.

Wagstaff, John. "Pension Application of John Wagstaff R10998." Southern Campaign American Revolution Pension Statements & Rosters. https://revwarapps.org/r10998.pdf.

Watson, William. "Pension Application of William Watson S17180." Southern Campaign American Revolution Pension Statements & Rosters. https://revwarapps.org/s17180.pdf.

Webb, John. "Pension Application of John Webb BLWt2052-450." Southern Campaign American Revolution Pension Statements & Rosters. https://revwarapps.org/blwt2052-450.pdf.

Websites

American Battlefield Trust. "George Weedon." https://www.battlefields.org.

American Revolution Experience. "George Weedon (1734–1793)." https://american-revolution-experience.battlefields.org.

Christ's College Cambridge Alumni. "Thomas Nelson Jnr. (1738–1789)." https://alumni.christs.cam.ac.uk.

Culpeper Minutemen Chapter, Virginia Society, Sons of the American Revolution. "History of the Culpeper Minutemen Battalion, 1775." https://sites.google.com/view/culpeperminutemen/culpeper-history.

Dabney Family of Early Virginia. "William Fontaine." https://www.dabney-early-virginia.info.

Douglas, Davison M. "St. George Tucker." Encyclopedia Virginia, last updated August 26, 2024. https://encyclopediavirginia.org.

Ebel, Carol. "George Mathews." New Georgia Encyclopedia, last updated September 11, 2014. https://www.georgiaencyclopedia.org.

Bibliography

Edmunds, Jeffrey Garth. "John Francis Mercer of Stafford County: A Neglected Patriot." *Librarypoint* (blog), Central Rappahannock Regional Library, June 14, 2022. https://www.librarypoint.org.
Find a Grave. "Capt. David Meriwether (1716–1772)." https://www.findagrave.com.
———. "Col. Charles Dabney (1745–1829)." https://www.findagrave.com.
———. "Gen. Robert Lawson (1748–1805)." https://www.findagrave.com.
———. "George West." https://www.findagrave.com.
———. "George William Grayson." https://www.findagrave.com.
———. "Hugh West." https://www.findagrave.com.
———. "John Brett Richeson." https://www.findagrave.com.
———. "John West." https://www.findagrave.com.
———. "LTC William Fontaine." https://www.findagrave.com.
———. "Sir John Peyton." https://www.findagrave.com.
Fore, Samuel K. "George Weedon." George Washington Presidential Library, Center for Digital History, George Washington's Mount Vernon. https://www.mountvernon.org.
Gruber, Drew. "Mercer's Grenadier Militia." *Emerging Civil War* (blog), July 29, 2015. https://emergingcivilwar.com.
Kingsmill on the James Community Services Association. "History of Kingsmill." https://www.kingsmillcommunity.org.
Loudoun County Museum. "Loudoun History." https://web.archive.org/web/20140324004622/http://www.loudounmuseum.org/loudoun-history.
Maryland Center for History and Culture. "Hors du Monde, the Home of Colonel Skipwith, Cumberland County, Virginia." https://www.mdhistory.org.
National Park Service. "Edward Stevens (1745–1820)." Last updated February 26, 2015. https://www.nps.gov.
Neville, Gabriel. "The 'Darke Side' of Washington." *8th Virginia Regiment* (blog), January 1, 2019. https://www.8thvirginia.com.
Southern Virginia Homefront. "MacCallum More Museum & Gardens: Remains of Stoneland Plantation & Nearby Civil War Trails Marker for Christianville at Butler Memorial Library." http://sovahomefront.org.
Sweet Springs Sanitarium. "Colonel William Lewis: The Original Founder of Sweet Springs Resort aka Sweet Springs Sanitarium." July 4, 2021. https://sweetspringssanitarium.wordpress.com.
Tarter, Brent. "William Darke (1736–1801)." Dictionary of Virginia Biography, Library of Virginia. https://www.lva.virginia.gov.

Bibliography

Tarter, Brent, and the Dictionary of Virginia Biography. "John Robinson (1705–1766)." Encyclopedia Virginia. Last updated December 22, 2021. https://encyclopediavirginia.org.

Thomas Jefferson's Monticello. "Reuben Lindsay (1747–1831)." Thomas Jefferson Encyclopedia. https://www.monticello.org.

Van Tol, Naomi. "Slaves of John Webb, Granville County, North Carolina." WikiTree. https://www.wikitree.com.

Webb, Richard. "Lt. Col. John Pomfret Webb." Webb Genealogy: Person Sheet. https://webbgenealogy.com.

William & Mary Libraries. "James Innes (1754–1798)." Special Collections Research Center Knowledgebase. https://scrcwiki.libraries.wm.edu.

———. "John Page (1744–1808)." Special Collections Research Center Knowledgebase. https://scrcwiki.libraries.wm.edu.

———. "St. George Tucker (1752–1827)." Special Collections Research Center Knowledgebase. https://scrc-kb.libraries.wm.edu.

Index

A

Abercrombie, Lieutenant Colonel Robert 34
Albemarle Barracks 45
American Colonization Society 76
Arnold, Brigadier General Benedict 33, 39, 45, 53, 57, 63, 67, 82, 89, 122

B

Baytop, Lieutenant Colonel James 27, 137, 139
Bermuda 34, 107, 112
Bland, Theodorick 108
Braddock, Major General Edward 37, 61, 65
Brandywine, Battle of 27, 38, 52, 56, 73, 78, 85, 102, 115, 120
Burwell, Anne (Spotswood) 30
Burwell, Colonel Lewis 30, 31, 137
Burwell, Elizabeth (Harrison) 31

C

Charleston, Siege of 18, 52, 60, 103, 116
Chesapeake-Leopold Affair 72
Choisy, Marquis de 123
Cincinnati, Society of the 28, 31, 34, 58, 68, 125, 139
College of William & Mary 45, 51, 73, 79, 87, 93, 107, 110
Cooch's Bridge, Battle of 38
Cornwallis, General Charles 33, 39, 44, 53, 57, 82, 103, 122, 130

D

Dabney, Captain George 36
Dabney, Colonel Charles 32, 34, 138, 139
Darke, Captain Joseph 41
Darke, Colonel William 37, 137, 139

Index

Darke, Sarah (Deleyea) 37
Dunmore, Lord (John Murray) 32, 51, 55, 87, 93, 101

E

Edmonds, Colonel Elias, Jr. 43, 44, 137, 139

F

Fontaine, Ann (Morris) 47
Fontaine, Lieutenant Colonel William 45, 138, 139
Franklin, Benjamin 54
Freemasonry 72, 75, 106, 125
French and Indian War 37, 43, 61, 65, 73, 95, 118, 120

G

Gates, Major General Horatio 39, 103
Germantown, Battle of 27, 32, 38, 52, 56, 67, 78, 103, 120
Gloucester Point 24, 31, 50, 53, 74, 89, 123, 128, 129
Gordon, William F. 64
Gosport Shipyard 70
Grand Lodge of Virginia 72
Grant, General Ulysses S. 97
Grayson, Colonel William 44
Great Bridge, Battle of 43, 70, 101
Greene, Major General Nathanael 57, 93, 99, 103, 120, 121
Griffin, Colonel Samuel 49, 86

Griffin, Colonel William 49, 123, 137
Griffin, Corbin 49
Griffin, Cyrus 50
Guilford Courthouse, Battle of 18, 57, 74, 93, 99, 104, 106

H

Hamilton, Lieutenant Colonel Henry 39
Harlem Heights, Battle of 49, 73, 119
Harrison, William Henry 31, 73
Henry, Patrick 30, 32, 52, 54, 80, 95
Hook, Battle of the 21, 74, 117, 125, 129, 135

I

Innes, Colonel James 51, 53, 82, 122, 137, 139
Innes, Elizabeth (Cocke) 52

J

Jackson, Lieutenant General Thomas "Stonewall" 36
Jackson, Major General Andrew 36
James I (king) 91, 98
Jefferson, Thomas 27, 30, 33, 39, 47, 57, 63, 67, 73, 81, 87, 89, 98, 104, 105, 119
Jouett, Jack 105

INDEX

K

Knox, Major General Henry 21, 34

L

Lafayette, Marquis de 33, 36, 53, 57, 74, 82, 99, 105, 108, 122
Lauzun, Duc de 74, 116, 122
Lawson, Brigadier General Robert 12, 24, 55, 56, 58, 68, 82, 96, 99, 104, 108, 130, 137, 139
Lee, Major General Charles 38, 49, 73
Leslie, Major General Alexander 56, 121
Lewis, Brigadier General Andrew 61, 66, 113
Lewis, Colonel William 19, 60, 62, 78, 138
Lewis, Meriwether 77
Lindsay, Colonel Reuben 63, 138
Lindsay, Sarah (Walker) 63

M

Madison, James 42, 64, 110, 111
Marshall, Colonel Thomas 43, 70
Marshall, John 36, 43, 72, 111
Maryland House of Delegates 75
Mathews, Brigadier General George 67, 68
Mathews, Colonel Sampson 65, 67, 68, 137
Mathews, Colonel Thomas 70, 72, 138, 139
Mathews, Mollie (Miller) 70
Maxwell, Brigadier General William 38
McClanahan, Colonel Alexander 115
Mercer, Brigadier General Hugh 52, 118, 120
Mercer, Lieutenant Colonel John Francis 21, 73, 75, 125, 135, 137, 139
Meriwether, Colonel Thomas 77, 78
Monroe, James 73, 90, 120
Morgan, Brigadier General Daniel 38, 39, 104
Muhlenberg, Major General Peter 38, 60, 67, 121

N

Nelson, Brigadier General Thomas, Jr. 12, 20, 21, 31, 45, 53, 68, 79, 82, 84, 88, 92, 109, 122, 137
Nelson, Colonel William 85
Nelson, Lucy (Chiswell) 85
Nelson, Lucy (Grymes) 80
Nelson, Thomas, Sr. 85

P

Page, Colonel John 27, 80, 87, 89, 123, 137
Page, Frances (Burwell) 87, 89
Peyton, Colonel Sir John 28, 91, 138
Phillips, Major General William 53, 122

Index

Point Pleasant, Battle of 66, 113
Princeton, Battle of 44, 52, 55, 120
Puller, Lieutenant General Lewis Burwell "Chesty" 31

R

Randolph, Colonel Beverley 93, 108, 137
Randolph, Edmund 94, 110
Randolph, John 108
Randolph, Martha (Cocke) 93
Richeson, Colonel Holt 95, 137, 139
Richeson, Elizabeth (Hogg) 95
Richeson, Susanna (West) 95
Roosevelt, Franklin D. 76
Rush, Benjamin 37
Rutherford, Lucy Mercer 76

S

Shenandoah Valley 11, 18, 38, 39, 60, 62, 65
Skipwith, Anne (Wayles) 98
Skipwith, Lieutenant Colonel Henry 98, 99, 137
Smallwood, Major General William 32
St. Clair, Major General Arthur 41
Stephen, Major General Adam 40, 58
Steuben, Baron Friedrich Wilhelm von 53, 81, 115
Stevens, Brigadier General Edward 12, 20, 40, 44, 57, 77, 82, 101, 102, 104, 137

Stevens, Gizzell "Gilly" (Coleman) 101
Stuart, Major General J.E.B. 36

T

Taliaferro, Brigadier General William Booth 29
Taliaferro, Colonel Lawrence 43, 101
Tarleton, Lieutenant Colonel Banastre 53, 104, 116
Trenton, Battle of 44, 49, 55, 119
Tucker, Frances (Bland Randolph) 108
Tucker, Lelia (Skipwith Carter) 110
Tucker, Lieutenant Colonel St. George 20, 100, 107, 108, 110, 138

U

University of Virginia 64
U.S. House of Representatives 50, 61, 68, 75, 77, 90
USS *Chesapeake* 72
U.S. Senate 111

V

Vance, Colonel Samuel 113, 114, 138
Vance, Sarah (Bird) 113, 114
Virginia Convention Guard 45
Virginia House of Burgesses 49, 80, 88, 93, 95

Virginia House of Delegates 28,
 40, 44, 53, 56, 58, 61, 68, 72,
 74, 83, 89, 93, 96, 100
Virginia Senate 67, 105

W

Wabash, Battle of the 41
Washington, Brigadier General
 William 73, 120
Washington, General George 24,
 30, 33, 37, 40, 41, 45, 49, 54,
 55, 63, 65, 70, 73, 80, 82, 85,
 94, 106, 108, 115, 118, 119,
 122, 125
Washington & Lee University 66
Waxhaws, Battle of the 18
Wayne, Major General Anthony
 33, 38
Webb, Amy (Booker) 115
Webb, Lieutenant Colonel John 53,
 115, 123, 138, 139
Weedon, Brigadier General George
 12, 20, 27, 31, 50, 53, 67, 74,
 82, 89, 92, 102, 116, 118,
 121, 123, 128, 137, 139
Weedon, Catherine "Kitty"
 (Gordon) 118, 125
Wirt, William 36
Woodford, Brigadier General
 William 101, 115, 120, 121
Wythe, George 51, 107, 110
Wythe House 82, 100

About the Author

Dr. Sean M. Heuvel is an administrator at Christopher Newport University in Newport News, Virginia, where he also served for over fifteen years as a faculty member. A military historian by training, Sean specializes primarily in the American Revolution and the Civil War. His edited and coauthored books include *The College of William & Mary in the Civil War* (McFarland, 2013), *The Revolutionary War Memoirs of Major General William Heath* (McFarland, 2014) and *From Across the Sea: North Americans in Nelson's Navy* (Helion and Company, 2020). Active in several hereditary and civic organizations, he also cofounded the Williamsburg/Yorktown American Revolution Roundtable in 2013. Sean holds a BA, MEd and PhD from The College of William & Mary and an MA from the University of Richmond. He lives in Williamsburg, Virginia, with his wife, Katey, and two children.